Contents

Chapter 1: How Governments Work

Democracy, monarchy and dictatorship: types of government systems	1
How government works	2
What is the role of Parliament in constitutional law?	4
The two-House system	5
How are laws made?	6
What does devolution in the United Kingdom mean?	7
Is the House of Commons losing the art of debate?	10
House of Lords: pros and cons of an unelected chamber	11
Why Parliament's mace is so important, and why an MP removed it from the House of Commons	12

Chapter 2: Voting & Democracy

From Magna Carta to universal suffrage, the 1000-year history of British democracy	14
Should we make voting compulsory?	16
Australian election: what is compulsory voting – and why is everyone talking about sausages?	17
Papers please: How the government is making it harder to vote in the local elections	18
Elections in Britain: why you should not vote	19
The people who can't vote in an election	20
Should the voting age be lowered to 16?	21
Three good reasons the voting age should be raised to 21 – not cut to 16	23
Voting systems in the UK	24
First past the post	26
Can democracy vote itself out of existence?	28
Ninety years since women got equal voting rights, these are the milestones we still need to aim for	30

Chapter 3: World Governments

Democracy in Retreat – *Freedom in the World 2019*	32
Ranked and mapped: which countries have the most women in parliament	34
Women's votes: six amazing facts from around the world	36
What type of government does the United States have?	37
United but different: differences and similarities between the US and the UK	38
The world's 6 most well-governed countries. Denmark, New Zealand, Canada, and Japan top 2018 BBC ranking	39

Key facts	40
Glossary	41
Activities	42
Index	43
Acknowledgements	44

Introduction

Government is Volume 360 in the ***ISSUES*** series. The aim of the series is to offer current, diverse information about important issues in our world, from a UK perspective.

ABOUT GOVERNMENT

A part of being a good citizen is having an understanding of how your country is governed and how your vote matters. In this book we explore how the UK Government is run, how laws are made and the importance of democracy. It also looks at other issues, such as different voting systems, and how our government compares to others around the world.

OUR SOURCES

Titles in the ***ISSUES*** series are designed to function as educational resource books, providing a balanced overview of a specific subject.

The information in our books is comprised of facts, articles and opinions from many different sources, including:

◆ Newspaper reports and opinion pieces

◆ Website factsheets

◆ Magazine and journal articles

◆ Statistics and surveys

◆ Government reports

◆ Literature from special interest groups.

A NOTE ON CRITICAL EVALUATION

Because the information reprinted here is from a number of different sources, readers should bear in mind the origin of the text and whether the source is likely to have a particular bias when presenting information (or when conducting their research). It is hoped that, as you read about the many aspects of the issues explored in this book, you will critically evaluate the information presented.

It is important that you decide whether you are being presented with facts or opinions. Does the writer give a biased or unbiased report? If an opinion is being expressed, do you agree with the writer? Is there potential bias to the 'facts' or statistics behind an article?

ACTIVITIES

In the back of this book, you will find a selection of activities designed to help you engage with the articles you have been reading and to explore your own opinions. Some tasks will take longer than others and there is a mixture of design, writing and research-based activities that you can complete alone or in a group.

FURTHER RESEARCH

At the end of each article we have listed its source and a website that you can visit if you would like to conduct your own research. Please remember to critically evaluate any sources that you consult and consider whether the information you are viewing is accurate and unbiased.

Useful Websites

www.apolitical.co

www.blogs.coventry.ac.uk

www.borgenproject.org

www.ceoworld.biz

www.electoral-reform.org.uk

www.foreignpolicynews.org

www.freedomhouse.org

www.gov.uk

www.independent.co.uk

www.inews.co.uk

www.news-decoder.com

www.parliament.uk

www.politics.co.uk

www.politicshome.com

www.telegraph.co.uk

www.theconversation.com

www.theweek.co.uk

www.worldatlas.com

Independence Educational Publishers

First published by Independence Educational Publishers

The Studio, High Green

Great Shelford

Cambridge CB22 5EG

England

Copyright

Photocopy licence

ISBN-13: 978 1 86168 816 3

Printed in Great Britain

Zenith Print Group

Democracy, monarchy and dictatorship: types of government systems

By Haley Hine

Aristotle was the first to define three principal types of government systems in the fourth century B.C. These consisted of monarchy, aristocracy and polity. Since then, many more have been formulated, but the main themes and ideas have remained. Today, the five most common government systems include democracy, republic, monarchy, communism and dictatorship. This list details what to know about each.

Five types of government systems

1. Democracy

A democracy can be defined as a government system with supreme power placed in the hands of the people. It can be traced back to as early as the fifth century B.C. In fact, the word democracy is Greek for 'people power'. While most use the United States as an example of a democratic government system, the United States actually has what is called a representative democracy. The difference lies in the method of civilian participation. In a direct democracy, every citizen is given an equal say in the government. In a representative democracy, citizens elect representatives who make the law. The difference is significant when put into action. Other examples of democratic states include Aruba, Bulgaria, Canada, Costa Rica and the Dominican Republic.

2. Republic

In a republic government system, the power also rests with the people, as they are in charge of electing or choosing the country's leader, instead of the leader being appointed or inheriting power. Broadly defined, a republic is a government system without a monarch. A republic may be governed by a group of nobles, as long as there is not a single monarch. Some examples of countries with a republic government system include Argentina, Bolivia, Czech Republic and France.

3. Monarchy

In a monarchy, state power is held by a single family that inherits rule from one generation to the next. In a monarchy, an individual from the royal family holds the position of power until they die. Today, the majority of monarchy governments have transitioned to constitutional monarchies, where the monarch is head of state but only performs ceremonial roles and does not have state power. Only a few countries still have systems where the monarch retains control; these include Brunei, Oman, Saudi Arabia and Swaziland.

4. Communism

A communist government system is usually based on a particular ideology of communism taught by Karl Marx or Vladimir Lenin. A single party or group of people usually runs communist states. In some cases, citizens of a communist state are given certain jobs or life duties in an effort to obtain collective citizenship for the state. Examples of communist states include China, Cuba and Vietnam.

5. Dictatorship

In a dictatorship, a single person, a dictator, has absolute power over the state. It is not necessarily ruled by a theology or belief. It is an authoritarian form of government where one person is in charge of enforcing and enacting the law. Aspects often include military organisational backing, unfair elections (if any) and various human rights violations. A dictator does not usually inherit their power like a monarch does; they either seize control of the state by force or through (usually unfair) elections. Dictators are not held accountable for their actions and thus are free to do as they please, including limiting citizens' rights. Burundi, Chad, Equatorial Guinea and North Korea are contemporary examples of countries run by a dictator.

While these types of government systems all vary, they have at least one similarity: the allocation of power. Whether it be the allocation of power to a single person, a group of people, or evenly distributed to everyone, power is the shared theme of all types of government systems.

20 May 2018

How government works

In the UK, the Prime Minister leads the government with the support of the Cabinet and ministers.

Who runs government

The Prime Minister

The Prime Minister is the leader of Her Majesty's Government and is ultimately responsible for all policy and decisions. The Prime Minister also:

◆ oversees the operation of the Civil Service and government agencies

◆ appoints members of the government

◆ is the principal government figure in the House of Commons.

The Cabinet

The Cabinet is made up of the senior members of government. Every week during Parliament, members of the Cabinet (Secretaries of State from all departments and some other ministers) meet to discuss the most important issues for the government.

Ministers

Ministers are chosen by the Prime Minister from the members of the House of Commons and House of Lords. They are responsible for the actions, successes and failures of their departments.

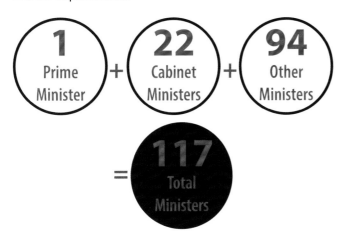

How government is run

Departments and their agencies are responsible for putting government policy into practice.

Government departments

Some departments, like the Ministry of Defence, cover the whole UK. Others don't – the Department for Work and Pensions doesn't cover Northern Ireland. This is because some aspects of government are devolved to Scotland, Wales and Northern Ireland.

Non-ministerial departments are headed by senior civil servants and not ministers. They usually have a regulatory or inspection function like the Charity Commission.

Executive agencies

These are part of government departments and usually provide government services rather than decide policy – which is done by the department that oversees the agency.

An example is the Driver and Vehicle Licensing Agency (overseen by the Department for Transport).

Other public bodies

These have varying degrees of independence but are directly accountable to ministers. There are four types of non-departmental public bodies (NDPBs).

Executive NDPBs do work for the government in specific areas - for example, the Environment Agency.

Advisory NDPBs provide independent, expert advice to ministers - for example, the Committee on Standards in Public Life.

Tribunal NDPBs are part of the justice system and have jurisdiction over a specific area of law – for example, the Competition Appeal Tribunal.

Independent monitoring boards are responsible for the running of prisons and treatment of prisoners – for example, Her Majesty's Inspectorate of Prisons.

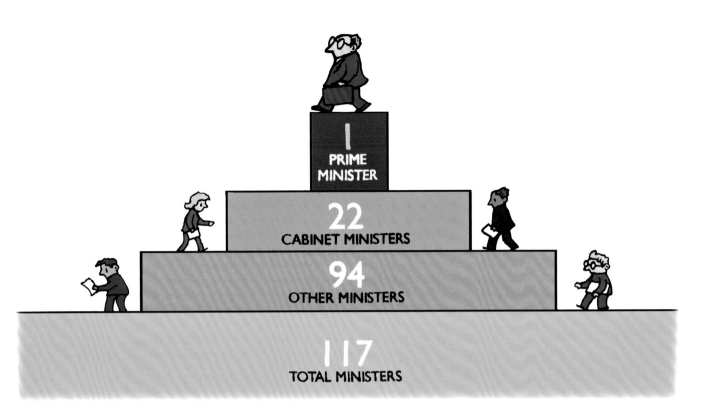

1 PRIME MINISTER

22 CABINET MINISTERS

94 OTHER MINISTERS

117 TOTAL MINISTERS

Civil Service

The Civil Service does the practical and administrative work of government. It is co-ordinated and managed by the Prime Minister, in their role as Minister for the Civil Service.

Around half of all civil servants provide services direct to the public, including:

◆ paying benefits and pensions

◆ running employment services

◆ staffing prisons

◆ issuing driving licences.

Legislation

Laws go through several stages before they are passed by Parliament. The House of Commons and the House of Lords work together to make them.

They can include:

Draft legislation

White papers outline proposals for new laws. Green papers ask for public comments before the white paper is published.

Bills are proposals for new laws or changes to existing ones. Once agreed by Parliament, they have to be approved by The Queen before becoming law.

Acts of Parliament

These are bills which have been approved by the Commons, the Lords, and The Queen. The relevant government department is responsible for putting the act into practice.

Devolved government

In Scotland, Wales and Northern Ireland, devolved administrations are responsible for many domestic policy issues, and their Parliaments/Assemblies have law-making powers for those areas.

Areas the Scottish Government, Welsh Government, and the Northern Ireland Executive are responsible for, include:

◆ health

◆ education

◆ culture

◆ the environment

◆ transport.

Local government

Councils make and carry out decisions on local services. Many parts of England have 2 tiers of local government: county councils and district, borough or city councils.

In some parts of the country, there's just one tier of local government providing all the functions, known as a 'unitary authority'. This can be a city, borough or county council – or it may just be called 'council'. As well as these, many areas also have parish or town councils.

Parliament

Parliament is separate from government. Made up of the House of Commons and the House of Lords, its role is to:

◆ look at what the government is doing

◆ debate issues and pass new laws

◆ set taxes

What is the role of Parliament in constitutional law?

You know that Parliament is important because when you visit London, you have to visit and get a selfie outside. You probably know that our elected MPs make the laws inside. Did you know that we have a British constitution? Parliament is one of the most important legal institutions in the UK with a wide variety of roles.

What is the composition of Parliament?

Parliament is formed of three main bodies. It is bicameral, which means that it has two houses in its seat in Westminster – the House of Commons and the House of Lords. The third body is its head – the Sovereign. The agreement of all three of these bodies is required for Parliament to pass a law.

The House of Commons consists of 650 elected MPs, who are accountable to their constituents who vote them into power at each election. In contrast, the House of Lords consists of unelected members, including hereditary peers that inherit their position, bishops of the Church of England and life peers appointed by the monarch and chosen by the government.

People often think that the government comes entirely from the House of Commons, but ministers can actually be drawn from both Houses.

What is constitutional law?

Parliament has a key role within constitutional law. This is the law that sets out how we govern our country and the rules that affect how different parts of government interact with each other and the people.

Most people don't know that we do actually have a constitution. Most people don't because it isn't in one place, like most constitutions in the world. Ours is called an uncodified constitution. It consists of a web of documents, stretching back to the Magna Carta in 1215 as well as our traditions and unwritten rules. Interestingly, we are one of only five countries in the world with uncodified constitutions – keeping company with Canada, Saudi Arabia, New Zealand and Israel.

Parliament is a central institution within our constitution.

What are the functions of Parliament?

The main function of Parliament is to pass laws on a variety of topics. Currently, Parliament debates, scrutinises and approves laws proposed by the government for England. They can also pass laws in some areas in other parts of the country such as Scotland, Wales and Northern Ireland. However, because these parts of the country have devolved Parliaments and Assemblies, some issues are governed locally.

For example, Scotland has the power to decide its laws on education, Wales can change its housing policies and Northern Ireland has control over health and social services. There is a long list of areas that these devolved parts of the UK have control over.

However, a key concept that underpins the role of Parliament in constitutional law is parliamentary sovereignty. This is the idea that it is the supreme law-making body in the UK. There is nothing higher than Parliament.

It can pool its sovereignty with other areas, such as the European Union and devolved administrations. Fundamentally, though, it can withdraw the sovereignty it hands out and has ultimate control.

However, Parliament does more than just pass laws. It has a key role of holding the government to account. For example, the Public Accounts Committee is a feared body that scrutinises the financial dealings of the government and summons ministers to answer for their spending. Parliament has the weighty job of approving government spending and taxation plans.

The government does have some power independent of Parliament though. The royal prerogative used to be the way that the monarch would exercise their power, though these days they do so only to fulfil the will of the Prime Minister. Key areas such as national security, war and defence are controlled under this constitutional law.

Finally, Parliament is a site of debate and this is a worthy function in its own right. It is a place where the nation looks to in times of crisis and major issues. For example, when wars in Iraq and Afghanistan were unfolding, parliamentary debate was a focus of attention, despite this falling under the prerogative of the government.

Parliament does not act alone. It is influenced by a whole range of factors, including public opinion, the government, pressure groups, the Royal Commission and the Law Commission. Nonetheless, it is one of the most significant institutions in our constitutional framework and affects all of us every day.

The above information is reprinted with kind permission from the Coventry University Group.
© 2019 Coventry University

www.blogs.coventry.ac.uk/discover/

The two-House system

The business of Parliament takes place in two Houses: the House of Commons and the House of Lords. Their work is similar: making laws (legislation), checking the work of the government (scrutiny), and debating current issues.

The House of Commons is also responsible for granting money to the government through approving Bills that raise taxes. Generally, the decisions made in one House have to be approved by the other.

In this way the two-chamber system acts as a check and balance for both Houses.

The Commons

The Commons is publicly elected. The party with the largest number of members in the Commons forms the government.

Members of the Commons (MPs) debate the big political issues of the day and proposals for new laws. It is one of the key places where government ministers, like the Prime Minister and the Chancellor, and the principal figures of the main political parties, work.

The Commons alone is responsible for making decisions on financial Bills, such as proposed new taxes. The Lords can consider these Bills but cannot block or amend them.

The Lords

The House of Lords is the second chamber of the UK Parliament. It is independent from, and complements the work of, the elected House of Commons. The Lords shares the task of making and shaping laws and checking and challenging the work of the government.

How are laws made?

One of Parliament's main roles is debating and passing laws.

Why are new laws needed?

New laws

The Government introduces most plans for new laws, with many included in the Queen's Speech at the opening of each session of Parliament, and changes to existing laws. However, new laws can originate from an MP or a Lord.

Emergency issues such as the threat of terrorism, pressure on the Government to update old laws and case law in the courts, interpreting, clarifying and re-applying established principles of statute law, all contribute to the need for new laws.

Who is consulted about changes to the law?

Before proposals for laws, known as Bills, are introduced into Parliament, there is often consultation or discussion with interested parties such as professional bodies, voluntary organisations and pressure groups.

White and Green Papers

Proposals for legislative changes may be contained in government White Papers. These may be preceded by consultation papers, sometimes called Green Papers, which set out government proposals that are still taking shape and seek comments from the public. There is no requirement for White or Green Papers to be introduced before a Bill is introduced into Parliament.

Draft Bills and pre-legislative scrutiny

A Draft Bill is a Bill that is published to enable consultation and pre-legislative scrutiny before a Bill is formally introduced into either the House of Commons or House of Lords.

A Draft Bill is considered, often by a departmental select committee in the Commons or by a joint committee of Lords and Members of the Commons. This allows MPs and Members of the Lords to have early influence on the Bill. This process is known as pre-legislative scrutiny.

Do all Bills apply to the whole of the UK?

Some Bills apply to the whole of the UK.

However, Bills may apply to one or more constituent parts – for example, only to England and Wales. Law-making powers in some subjects rest with the Scottish Parliament, the Welsh Assembly and the Northern Ireland Assembly, rather than the UK Parliament.

International and EU legislation

Sometimes new laws are also needed to ensure that the UK complies with international or EU legislation.

What is a Draft Bill?

Draft Bills are issued for consultation before being formally introduced to Parliament. This allows proposed changes to be made before the Bill's formal introduction. Almost all Draft Bills are Government Bills. Government departments produce Draft Bills and issue them to interested parties. MPs and Lords can also consider them in committees.

Why are there Draft Bills?

The practice of publishing Draft Bills has become more frequent in recent years. It allows examination and amendments to be made to texts and made more easily - before their formal introduction to Parliament as a Bill proper.

Parliament's role in Draft Bills

Most Draft Bills are examined either by select committees in the Commons or Lords or by a joint committee of both Houses.

Government's role in Draft Bills

The consultation process on Draft Bills may involve the government issuing a paper for public discussion and response. The best-known examples of this are White and Green Papers.

Although not formal definitions, Green Papers usually put forward ideas for future government policy that are open to public discussion and consultation. White Papers generally state more definite intentions for government policy.

What is a bill?

A Bill is a proposal for a new law, or a proposal to change an existing law that is presented for debate before Parliament.

Bills are introduced in either the House of Commons or House of Lords for examination, discussion and amendment.

When both Houses have agreed on the content of a Bill it is then presented to the reigning monarch for approval (known as Royal Assent).

Once Royal Assent is given, a Bill becomes an Act of Parliament and is law.

Different types of Bills can be introduced by:

- The government
- Individual MPs or Lords
- Private individuals or organisations.

There are three different types of Bill: Public, Private and Hybrid Bills.

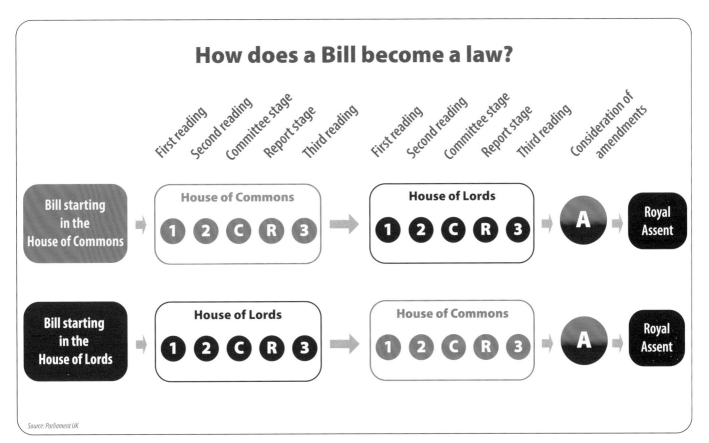

How does a Bill become a law?

First reading · Second reading · Committee stage · Report stage · Third reading

Bill starting in the House of Commons → House of Commons 1 2 C R 3 → House of Lords 1 2 C R 3 → A → Royal Assent

Bill starting in the House of Lords → House of Lords 1 2 C R 3 → House of Commons 1 2 C R 3 → A → Royal Assent

First reading · Second reading · Committee stage · Report stage · Third reading · Consideration of amendments

Source: Parliament UK

How does a bill become a law?

Guide to the passage of a Bill

A Bill is a proposal for a new law, or a proposal to change an existing law, presented for debate before Parliament.

A Bill can start in the Commons or the Lords and must be approved in the same form by both Houses before becoming an Act (law).

What is an Act of Parliament?

An Act of Parliament creates a new law or changes an existing law. An Act is a Bill that has been approved by both the House of Commons and the House of Lords and been given Royal Assent by the Monarch. Taken together, Acts of Parliament make up what is known as Statute Law in the UK.

Putting the Act into force

The Government are responsible for bringing new laws into force, once they has been passed by Parliament.

An Act may come into force immediately, on a specific future date, or in stages. You can find out when an Act is due to come into force by looking at a section of the Act itself, headed 'Commencement' – this is among the very last sections of an Act.

Sometimes a specific date is not given and the timing is left to the discretion of the Secretary of State for the relevant government department.

Although Parliament is not responsible for implementing legislation, its committees can investigate how well an Act is being implemented by the Government and the effect that the new law is having. This is known as post-legislative scrutiny.

Changes to Acts

Future changes to the law happen through the passing of another Act or delegated legislation. An Act can also be repealed so that its provisions no longer apply. Parliamentary committees examine UK laws and recommend the removal of out-of-date legislation.

Writing of Acts

The UK Houses of Parliament changed from hand writing original Acts of Parliament to printing them in 1849. They are printed on vellum, and still are to this day.

The Acts were also the bills, until the switch to printing. The bills would pass through one House, be handwritten onto parchment after report stage, and all amendments made on third reading and during all stages in the second House were painstakingly made onto the parchment. This same document became the Act after Royal Assent. This is the case from 1497–1849, so anyone wanting to consult bills in this period should actually consult the original Act.

There do additionally exist printed Bills for reference from the early 18th century but they weren't made systematically, there's no definitive set here, sometimes they were printed by private promoters (rather than by Parliament), and where odd Bills do survive there's often no indication of what stage of debate they were made at. Their usefulness therefore varies.

What is Secondary Legislation?

Secondary legislation is law created by ministers (or other bodies) under powers given to them by an Act of Parliament.

It is used to fill in the details of Acts (primary legislation). These details provide practical measures that enable the law to be enforced and operate in daily life.

Secondary legislation can be used to set the date for when provisions of an Act will come into effect as law, or to amend existing laws.

For example, governments often use secondary legislation to ban new substances in response to new information about their dangers by adding them to a list under the Misuse of Drugs Act 1971.

Statutory Instruments

Statutory Instruments (SIs) are documents drafted by a government department to make changes to the law. They are published with an explanatory memorandum, which outlines the purpose of the SI and why the change is necessary.

SIs are the most frequently used type of secondary legislation, with approximately 3,500 made each year, although only about 1,000 need to be considered by Parliament.

They usually have either rule, order or regulation in their title.

Parliament's role

Parliament can either approve or reject an SI, but cannot amend it. Parliament's role in considering an SI varies depending on what is stated in its parent Act.

The Joint Committee on Statutory Instruments (JCSI) checks SIs to make sure the law they contain is clear and follows the powers given by the parent Act.

If the JCSI identifies an issue, they publish recommendations on the SI. In the House of Lords, affirmative SIs cannot be debated before the JCSI make their recommendations.

The JCSI generally only takes evidence from the government department who wrote the SI. They can consider submissions from the public but only on points of law.

The Parliament Acts

The powers of the House of Lords are limited by a combination of law and convention.

The Parliament Acts, although rarely used, provide a way of solving disagreement between the Commons and the Lords.

Parliament Acts: background

Until the early years of the 20th century, the House of Lords had the power to veto (stop) legislation.

However, this arrangement was put under pressure when the House of Lords refused to pass David Lloyd-George's 'people's budget' of 1909. Eventually, the budget was passed after a general election in 1910; a second general election was then fought on the issue of reform of the House of Lords.

Parliament Act 1911

The result was the Parliament Act 1911, which removed from the House of Lords the power to veto a Bill, except one to extend the lifetime of a Parliament. Instead, the Lords could delay a Bill by up to two years. The Act also reduced the maximum life span of a Parliament from seven years to five years.

Parliament Act 1949

The Parliament Act 1949 further reduced the Lords' delaying powers to one year.

The Parliament Acts define the powers of the Lords in relation to Public Bills as follows.

Money Bills

Money Bills (Bills designed to raise money through taxes or spend public money) start in the Commons and must receive Royal Assent no later than a month after being introduced in the Lords, even if the Lords has not passed them. The Lords cannot amend Money Bills.

Other Commons Bills

Most other Commons Bills can be held up by the Lords if they disagree with them for about a year but ultimately the elected House of Commons can reintroduce them in the following session and pass them without the consent of the Lords.

Bills not subject to the Parliament Acts

- Bills prolonging the length of a Parliament beyond five years
- Private Bills
- Bills sent up to the Lords less than a month before the end of a session
- Bills which start in the Lords.

Bills subject to the Parliament Acts

Only seven Bills have become Acts under this procedure:

- Government of Ireland Act 1914
- Welsh Church Act 1914
- Parliament Act 1949
- War Crimes Act 1991
- European Parliament Elections Act 1999
- Sexual Offences (Amendment) Act 2000
- Hunting Act 2004.

The above information is reprinted with kind permission from Parliament UK.
© Crown copyright 2019

www.parliament.uk

What does devolution in the United Kingdom mean?

Devolution refers to the statutory granting of powers from the UK Parliament to the governments of the countries of the UK.

Devolution is a process of decentralising the government and giving more power to the local administration. Since 1999 the UK has been devolved its powers to Wales, Scotland and Northern Ireland, which alongside England makes up the United Kingdom. In the UK, devolution means the transfer of power and decision making from the UK parliament in London to the assemblies in the respective countries.

Background to devolution

In September 1997, Wales and Scotland held referendums to establish the National Assembly for Wales and the Scottish Parliament. A majority voted for the establishment of the two assemblies. In May 1998, Northern Ireland also held the referendum, and a majority voted in favour. Following the endorsements, the UK parliament passed the Northern Ireland Act 1998, the Scotland Act 1998, and the Government of Wales Act 1998. The latter was later superseded by the Government of Wales Act 2006. The three legislatures possess some powers previously held at Westminster. The UK power retained the power to amend the acts and legislate on any issue arising from devolution with the consent of the devolved legislatures. There are several differences between the parliament and the devolved legislatures; among them is how members are elected to either house. Members of parliament are elected based on first-past-the-post while members of the devolved legislatures are elected based on proportional representation.

Devolved administrations

Just like how the government is formed by members of the two Houses of Parliament, the developed legislatures nominate ministers to the executives referred to as the devolved administrations. The Scottish government consists of majority members of the Scottish National Party. The Welsh government is formed by the labour party while the Northern Ireland Executive is formed by a coalition of five parties. The official of the administrations do not serve the UK government and are not answerable to the Prime Minister. They are answerable to their own ministers and work to fulfil their territorial priorities and mandates. Within the UK government, Wales, Northern Ireland, and Scotland are each represented by a territorial secretary of state who ensures that the devolution between the government and the administrations are running smoothly.

In 2012, an MOU was agreed upon by the devolved administration and the UK government. The Memorandum set out the principles that support the coexistence of the administrations. The principles focus on good and open communication, co-operation and consultation. The MOU was accompanied by an agreement by the Joint Ministerial

Committee which provided protocols on avoidance and resolution of conflicts, international relations, concordats on the coordination of EU policies, and Financial assistance.

Some of the core functions devolved include agriculture, education, health, housing, local governments, and transportation. Powers still held by the government include security, the constitution, energy, immigration, pension, foreign, and policy. Some issues such as taxation remain contentious among the devolved governments and the government. The Brexit vote has left the UK divided after England and Wales voted in favour while Scotland and Northern Ireland voted against leaving the EU.

26 January 2018

Is the House of Commons losing the art of debate?

The Commons chamber is about exchange, back and forth, argument and counter-argument. But ever stricter time-limits, and speeches read from scripts are putting that tradition at risk.

By Tony Grew

'Too much of our Parliament isn't debate, it's speeches,' Tom Tugendhat observed recently. 'It's like line dancing. You may be with others in the same room but fundamentally you are dancing alone.'

In December and January, we had long debates on the withdrawal agreement. Speaker Bercow is keen to accommodate colleagues and likes to fit everyone in. This leads to MPs being put on a three-minute time limit, or in some cases a two- or one-minute limit. Is that really long enough to develop your point or to make a substantive argument?

The balance between hearing from as many MPs as possible or disappointing some to allow others a meaningful amount of time to speak, is a difficult one, but it goes to the heart of what debate is for.

The concept of limiting speaking times is relatively new. The first experiments happened in the 1980s and the first standing order providing for limits was made permanent in 1988. In 1995 some MPs thought a ten-minute limit was a bridge too far, but the standing orders were changed to give the Speaker that power.

Long-serving MPs have been known to lament the loss of oratorical skill in the Commons. Until recently only MPs at the despatch box were allowed to read out speeches, and MPs would shout 'reading!' at colleagues who relied too heavily on notes. Today it is not uncommon to see MPs read out not just speeches but questions and even interventions.

It is an unfortunate indication of a decline in the art of debating. How is it possible that someone cannot make a brief point on an intervention without writing it down first? A mix of unhelpfully short time limits and changes to the amount of injury time MPs get for allowing interventions has led to Mr Tugendhat's dance-based critique.

Allowing injury time for multiple interventions was designed to encourage spontaneous debate. In September the procedure committee declared that to be 'too generous' and recommended changes for speeches of more than five minutes, to reduce injury time to one minute for the first intervention. These changes were approved by the House.

Where a time limit of five minutes or lower is imposed the clock will not be stopped for any intervention and no injury time added. This seems contradictory. MPs are being encouraged not to take interventions, which is the point of a debate, a free flow of ideas.

At the same time as many speakers as possible are being crammed into the debate, so they can read out their points, which have often been made repeatedly by other MPs.

There is a balance to be struck between the 'all must speak' approach favoured by the Speaker or an alternative where only some MPs get in but have longer to expand their points and to take multiple interventions. Debate is not a demonstration of the ability to read out a prepared text. That is the practice in other parliaments and it's one of the reasons they are dull as ditchwater.

The Commons is about exchange, back and forth, argument and counter argument. We see this is alive and well when it comes to frontbenchers when they open a debate. They are unrestrained by limits on time or on the number of interventions they can take, and a confident minister or shadow minister will revel in the challenge.

Last week's Brexit debate was a masterclass in intervention. Yvette Cooper scored three in a row from the Prime Minister. 'I am simply trying to understand what she is saying,' she explained. Jeremy Corbyn showed us how not taking an intervention can overshadow your speech to such an extent that cabinet ministers are intervening to mock you for not taking an intervention.

The Prime Minister took 29 interventions in a 48-minute speech, from opponents on both sides of the House. Labour, SNP, DUP and Green MPs were able to engage her in debate. Lady Hermon, whose interventions are the weapon of choice of an excessively polite assassin, also got a chance to put her point forcefully on the record.

This makes for invigorating debate, it makes it easier for people watching to understand the issues at hand. People notice when questions aren't answered.

Nobody wants to return to the days when MPs could speak as long as they liked. Time limits are vital in order to regulate debate, as anyone who has had the misfortune to attend to Friday business will know.

But the procedure committee's recommendation that there should not be anything below a five-minute limit should be implemented. It may mean fewer MPs get to make a speech, but it might mean more interventions, which are surely more effective than Members demonstrating that they can read aloud.

4 February 2019

House of Lords: pros and cons of an unelected chamber

The Brexit debate has brought fresh scrutiny to the role of Parliament's upper chamber.

A petition to hold a referendum on scrapping the House of Lords has reached more than 150,000 signatures, meaning the issue will be debated in the House of Commons on 18 June.

'It could spell the end of almost 700 years of unelected peers wielding power in Britain,' says the *Daily Express*.

The upper chamber has faced criticism from Brexiteers in recent weeks after a series of striking defeats for the government's EU withdrawal bill.

Foreign Secretary Boris Johnson was among those to urge peers to respect the result of the EU referendum, saying 'they shouldn't frustrate it under any circumstances because they do not represent the sovereign will of the British people'.

The petition, set up by Robert McBride, calls for a referendum on the abolition of the chamber.

'The House of Lords is a place of patronage where unelected and unaccountable individuals hold a disproportionate amount of influence and power which can be used to frustrate the elected representatives of the people,' says McBride.

Reform of the Lords has been mooted but ultimately shelved many times in the past.

Now the Brexit debate has put it back in the public spotlight. So what do peers do and should they have a place in a modern democracy?

Who sits in the House of Lords?

The chamber currently has 665 eligible life peers, appointed by the Queen on the advice of the Prime Minister. It also has 90 hereditary peers and 26 bishops.

The Conservatives have the highest number of peers (244), although no majority, followed by Labour (188) and the Lib Dems (98) and a handful from minor parties, as well as 181 crossbenchers who are not affiliated with any party. High-profile appointments in the past few years have included Alan Sugar, star of *The Apprentice*, and Doreen Lawrence, mother of murdered teenager Stephen Lawrence.

Members meet in Westminster and are expected to scrutinise bills approved by the House of Commons. While they cannot normally prevent laws from being passed, they can delay bills and add on amendments that are then sent back for consideration in the House of Commons.

How much are peers paid?

Peers are not paid a salary but can claim a flat daily allowance of £150 or £300 if they attend a sitting.

The fresh scrutiny brought about by Brexit has also resurrected interest in the peers' allowance. One notorious anecdote reported in 2017 told of a peer who 'left the taxi running' outside the chamber while he dashed in to claim his £300, according to the *Daily Telegraph*.

Lady D'Souza, who stepped down as speaker of the upper chamber in 2016, told BBC documentary *Meet the Lords* that many of her colleagues did nothing to justify their stipend.

'There is a core of peers who work incredibly hard, who do that work, and there are, sad to say, many, many, many peers who contribute absolutely nothing but who claim the full allowance.'

What's wrong with the current system?

With nearly 800 peers, the House of Lords is the world's second-largest decision-making body after China's National People's Congress. Campaigners such as the Electoral Reform Society argue that it is undemocratic that unelected peers should have such sway in British politics.

A recent ICM poll for the pro-Brexit group Change Britain found that '43 percent of respondents would be more likely to back abolition or reform of the second chamber' if the House of Lords attempts to obstruct Brexit, reports *The Scotsman*, 'compared to 12 percent who are less likely'.

Former Labour leader Ed Miliband has also argued that the House of Lords as it stands 'fails to represent large parts of the UK'. For example, the north-west of England has nearly the same population as London but the capital has five times more members in the House of Lords.

What's right about the House of Lords?

In 2014, the *Daily Telegraph*'s Peter Oborne argued that the House of Lords continues to work remarkably well, throwing out what he calls 'populist measures introduced by governments determined to bolster their right-wing credentials'.

An elected House of Lords would never have the will or the courage to stand out against public opinion, he argues, and would deprive the public of the judgement of 'very valuable' peers, such as retired generals, trade union leaders, academics and judges.

'These are people with immense expertise, an important counterbalance to the Commons,' he says.

What are the alternatives?

All the main parties have pledged to cut the number of peers, and many politicians agree that hereditary peers should be phased out.

Ed Miliband previously proposed a wholly elected senate, with roughly proportionate numbers from Scotland, Wales, Northern Ireland and the English regions, instead of MP-style constituencies.

Four years ago, the Lib Dems put forward a proposal to halve the total number of members and ensure that at least 80 percent of peers were elected, but the plans were abandoned after an agreement with Tory opponents failed to be reached.

10 May 2018

Why Parliament's mace is so important, and why an MP removed it from the House of Commons

Without the mace, Parliament cannot lawfully meet, debate or pass laws.

By Serina Sandhu

In brief

- **A Labour MP grabbed the mace in protest over the Government's handling of Brexit**

- **The mace is a symbol of authority and removing it is deeply frowned upon**

It was chaos in the House of Commons on Monday night – and not just because of tense Brexit debating.

MPs could not believe their eyes when Labour's Lloyd Russell-Moyle grabbed the ceremonial mace in protest at the Government's handling of Brexit.

Describing it as a 'spur of the moment' act, the MP for Brighton Kemptown said he was protesting because the Tories were riding 'roughshod over the principle of parliamentary democracy' by pulling the 'meaningful vote'.

He carried the five-foot mace, which is a historic symbol of authority in the House of Commons, towards the doors before he was stopped by officials. The mace was then carried back to its rightful place on the table.

Shouts of 'disgrace' could be heard from MPs as the scandalous scene unfolded before their very eyes.

What is the mace?

The silver-gilt mace, decorated with roses and thistles springing from a stem entwined by a plain spiral ribbon, dates back to the 17th century and is believed to have been made for Charles II.

According to the Parliament website, it 'is the symbol of royal authority' within the chamber. Without its presence in the chamber, Parliament cannot lawfully meet, debate or pass laws. This rule also dates back to the 17th century.

On each day that the Commons is sitting, the mace is carried to the Chamber at the head of the Speaker's procession by the Serjeant at Arms, who is responsible for security and keeping order within the Commons. It is placed on the Table

Standing Order 43

'The Speaker, or the chairman, shall order any Member or Members whose conduct is grossly disorderly to withdraw immediately from the House during the remainder of that day's sitting; and the Serjeant at Arms shall act on such orders as he may receive from the chair in pursuance of this order. But if on any occasion the Speaker, or the chairman, deems that his powers under the previous provisions of this order are inadequate, he may name such Member or Members, in which event the same procedure shall be followed as is prescribed by Standing Order No. 44 (Order in debate).'

Source: iNews

of the House in front of the Speaker. At the end of the day it is carried out and returned to St James' Palace.

However, when the Commons sits as a committee, the mace is under the table.

The House of Lords uses two maces.

What are the consequences of removing the mace?

For an MP to remove the mace suggests the Government does not have the mandate to govern.

Under parliamentary rules it is seen as disorderly conduct. Speaker John Bercow can order MPs to leave the chamber for 'the remainder of the day'.

In his telling off of Mr Russell-Moyle, Mr Bercow said he had to suspend him according to number 43 of the Standing Orders of the House of Commons, which are written rules regulating the proceedings.

Why did the MP remove it?

The Labour MP said he was frustrated by the Government unilaterally deciding to ditch a vote using a solitary whip to order it to be postponed.

'I thought, one person is shouting "tomorrow" and literally hundreds of people are shouting "today", and the will of Parliament is going to be ignored,' said Mr Russell-Moyle.

'The symbolic gesture of lifting the mace and removing it is that the will of Parliament to govern is no longer, it has been removed, and I felt Parliament had effectively given up its sovereign right to govern properly.

'If we don't sort out our constitutional settlement so that governments can't do this in the future we do need to keep lodging these protests.'

Speaking of what happened after, Mr Russell-Moyle said: 'I was escorted out of Parliament by one of the men in tights who said 'all I would advise you, sir, is to try not to bring Parliament into disrepute again'.

'They were very nice about it but firm, "you've got to leave now" – I was always willing to hand it over and my intention was to walk outside and hand it over.

'But they stopped me before I got out of the chamber and I wasn't going to struggle with someone wearing a huge sword on their hip.'

How did people react?

MPs clearly saw the mace-grabbing as a disgraceful act. They called for the Speaker to 'expel' Mr Russell-Moyle.

Others saw the funny side of it.

The significance of the mace-grabbing definitely did not escape the US, judging by the country's headlines.

12 December 2018

From Magna Carta to universal suffrage, the 1000-year history of British democracy

By Tom Chivers

1215: Magna Carta

'The Great Charter' is most famous for consolidating judicial rights, notably habeas corpus, the right not to be unlawfully imprisoned.

However, it was also an important first step in removing power from the central authority – King John – and spreading it wider.

Its 61st clause, known as the Security Clause, declared that a council of 25 barons be created with the power to overrule the will of the King, by force if necessary.

This was repealed angrily by the King shortly afterwards, and mediaeval rulers largely ignored the document altogether, but it became an early foundation of England's – and later the United Kingdom's – unwritten constitution.

1376: The first Speaker of the House of Commons is appointed

An English Parliament had existed since late in the 13th century, and had been divided into two houses since 1341, with knights and burgesses sitting in what became known as the House of Commons, while clergy and nobility sat in the House of Lords.

However, its duties largely consisted of ratifying taxes for the Crown. In 1376, Thomas de la Mare was appointed to go to the King with complaints about taxation, and the Commons for the first time impeached some of the King's ministers.

While de la Mare was imprisoned for his actions, the House created the position of Speaker to represent the Commons permanently.

1688: The Great Revolution

The Civil War a few years before had removed the monarchy, and then reinstated it in a weakened form, setting the stage for the attenuated 'constitutional monarchy' that we have today.

But it was the arrival of William of Orange from Holland to take the throne from James II which led to the creation of the Bill of Rights, constitutionally preventing absolute rule by the Kings and Queens of Great Britain to this day, and leaving Parliament as the true seat of power in the country.

1832: The Reform Act

Democracy of sorts had existed in England for centuries – as far back as 1432, Henry VI passed statutes declaring who was eligible to vote (male owners of land worth at least 40 shillings, or a freehold property – perhaps half a million people nationwide).

However, the counties and boroughs that sent Members to Parliament were of wildly differing size.

The county of Yorkshire had more than 20,000 people, and the borough of Westminster had around 12,000, but they only sent one representative to the Commons – as did, for example, Dunwich, which had 32 voters, or Gatton, which had seven.

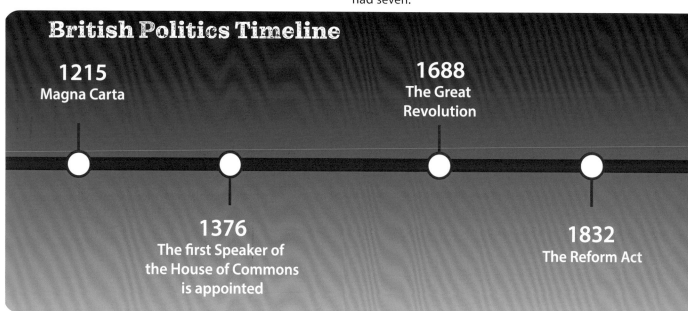

British Politics Timeline

1215
Magna Carta

1376
The first Speaker of the House of Commons is appointed

1688
The Great Revolution

1832
The Reform Act

The Reform Act increased enfranchisement to over a million, or about one in six of all adult males, by allowing men who rented property above a certain value to vote too.

It also tore up the mediaeval boundaries of counties and boroughs, giving more equitable representation for the cities that had sprung up since the Industrial Revolution. A second Act, in 1837, enfranchised all male householders, regardless of value.

1913: Emily Davison's 'Derby' death

Campaigns for women's suffrage go as far back as 1817, when the utilitarian philosopher Jeremy Bentham wrote *Plan of Parliamentary Reform*, in the form of a Catechism.

William Thompson and Anna Wheeler also published a pamphlet in 1825 on the subject.

However, despite these green shoots of support, the 1832 Act for the first time explicitly limited suffrage to 'male persons'.

It was not until 1861, when John Stuart Mill published *The Subjection of Women*, that the movement began to gain momentum.

In 1893, New Zealand became the first self-governing country to allow women to vote. In Britain, progress was slower, and in the early 20th century women took to direct and sometimes violent action; chaining themselves to railings, arson attacks, and even bombings.

Many were imprisoned, and some went on hunger strike. Emily Davison died at the Epsom Derby in 1913, when she ran out in front of the King's horse, Anmer, clutching the banner of the Women's Social and Political Union. It was around this time that the originally derogatory word 'suffragette' was coined, in a *Daily Mail* article.

1918: The Representation of the People Act

World War I could not be said to have had many silver linings, but it gave British women – who had spent the last four years, in a country shorn of young men, keeping the war effort running in munition factories and farms – a newfound political confidence.

The 1918 Act recognised that not only these women, but many soldiers who had supposedly fought for British democracy, were still unable to vote.

It removed all property restrictions from male voters, and allowed women to vote for the first time – although not those under 30, and with property restrictions – and to stand for election. The first woman, Nancy Astor, was elected to Parliament just 18 months later, in Plymouth Sutton. Ten years later, the restrictions on women were lifted, allowing them to vote at 21 whether or not they held property.

1969: The Representation of the People Act

After one final loophole was closed in 1948 – weirdly, up until that point, some seven percent of the electorate had two votes per person – voting in the United Kingdom reached essentially its modern state in 1969, when Harold Wilson's government dropped the voting age for all citizens from 21 to 18.

Further acts in 1983, 1985 and 2000 changed the laws on prisoners and overseas voters (essentially, convicted criminals may not vote while in prison; expatriates can still vote in their last constituency for 15 years after they left the country, and holidaymakers can vote by postal ballot or proxy).

In 2000, a hoary constitutional prejudice against 'lunatics' was weakened when psychiatric hospitals were allowed to be designated as registration addresses.

7 June 2017

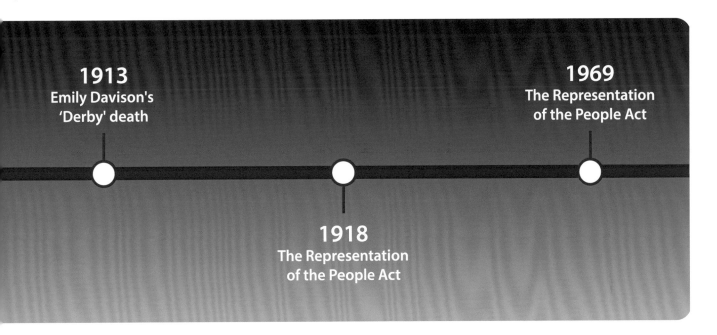

1913
Emily Davison's 'Derby' death

1918
The Representation of the People Act

1969
The Representation of the People Act

Should we make voting compulsory?

By Lizzie Lawless

Elections with low turnout are not uncommon in the UK, so it's only natural that questions are often raised on how we can see more voters heading to the ballot box.

Some argue that the key to higher turnout is to simply introduce compulsory voting. Since compulsory voting was introduced to Australia in 1924, turnout has never dropped below 91 percent. While compulsory voting may mask the symptoms, it isn't a cure for the disease.

The real problem is members of the public not wanting to vote. Many people who choose not to, do so because they feel their vote is powerless. And under the current Westminster voting system, they would be right.

With each constituency having just one MP to represent it, all votes cast for losing candidates are discarded. Additionally, all votes for an MP above what they need to win are wasted too – they do not count towards the final result. Whether an MP wins by one vote or 30,000 it makes no difference under Westminster's voting system.

> *'Forcing people to vote won't tackle the causes of low turnout, merely the symptoms.'*

In the 2017 General Election there were 22 million wasted votes – or 68% of the total. The result is that a party's support is often wildly misrepresented in the number of Commons' seats won.

What's more, in hundreds of seats across the country, people already know the result. In Britain's many 'safe seats', an election's outcome is sadly a foregone conclusion.

Why would you turn out to vote when you knew your vote would make no difference? Forcing people to turn out and fining those who do not vote won't suddenly make their vote matter.

Therefore, it's no surprise turnout currently suffers as a result – when people's interests are ignored, they become apathetic. Forcing people to vote won't tackle the causes of low turnout, merely the symptoms.

But it doesn't have to be this way. Outside of Westminster, most ways of electing parliaments don't involve wasting so many votes. With a fair proportional system, every vote makes a difference, and parties can no longer dominate for decades without real challenge. The number of seats can actually reflect how people vote.

What else can be done?

In the short term there are plenty of ways to make voting easier.

This could include: introducing voting on various days of the week, rather than just Thursdays; setting up voting stations in convenient public places such as supermarkets, local libraries and railway stations; introducing mobile polling stations to bring the ballot box closer to people, particularly in rural areas; and improve political and citizen education in schools. We can also make it easier to register to vote.

Rather than lowering barriers to citizens' participation and engagement, the government in Westminster is actually trying to make it harder to vote – the upcoming voter ID trials in 10 local authorities will prevent people without the right ID from casting a vote at the polling station. This is the exact opposite of what we should be doing. Thankfully, both the Welsh and Scottish governments have opened consultations on electoral reform recently and we discussed some of the options in our responses.

Compulsory voting may mask the symptoms, but a fairer voting system that gives voters a voice, automatic registration, and a better provision of information and citizenship education will help to solve the real underlying problem.

5 April 2019

Australian election: what is compulsory voting – and why is everyone talking about sausages?

Trend for buying sausages at election polls takes off across country.

By Abby Young-Powell

Australians have voted for the country's next leader. The general election, which will determine the nation's sixth Prime Minister in as many years, has been closely-fought between the conservative Liberal Party, led by current Prime Minister Scott Morrison, and Labor, led by Bill Shorten.

Opinion polls have predicted a win for the opposition, which would mean Mr Morrison, who only became Prime Minister in August, will have had one of the shortest tenures in the role in the 118-year history of the Australian federation.

By law Australians must vote. We take a look at Australia's system of mandatory voting, how and whether it works; and investigate why everyone's suddenly tweeting about sausages.

What is compulsory voting?

Since 1924 Australians have been legally required to enrol to vote in national elections, following a fall in turnout at the 1922 federal election. They are fined $20 if they fail to turn up. As a result, turnout has been as high as 96 percent in some elections and has never dropped below 91 percent since mandatory voting was introduced, according to CNN.

Australia is one of only 19 countries out of 166 electoral democracies to make voting compulsory, and is the only English-speaking country to do so.

Is mandatory voting considered a good thing?

Some say it infringes on an individual's right to abstain from voting. However, many argue in favour of it. In 2015, former US President Barack Obama floated the idea that other countries should adopt 'transformative' mandatory voting, too.

It would 'counteract money more than anything,' he said. 'The people who tend not to vote are young, they're lower income, they're skewed more heavily towards immigrant groups and minority groups,' Mr Obama said. 'There's a reason why some folks try to keep them away from the polls.'

In her book, *From Secret Ballot to Democracy Sausage*, Judith Brett argues compulsory voting has shielded Australia from political polarisation like that which has arguably infected politics in the United States and the UK.

What have sausages got to do with it?

Australians who headed to the polls to vote on Saturday could snag themselves a literal 'democracy sausage' to

eat. Over recent years, the trend for buying food – mainly sausages – at pop-up stalls outside polling booths has taken off.

Compulsory voting means large numbers of people are guaranteed to turn up to vote, providing an ample fundraising opportunity. That, along with a law which says polling day must always fall on a Saturday, has made the democracy sausage a rite of passage.

This year, the democracy sausage has also gone digital, with Australians posting photos under the Twitter hashtag #DemocracySausage and maps springing up to map local sausage stalls. Plus it's gone international, with sausages at polling booths as far away as New York, Berlin and Japan.

18 May 2019

Papers please: How the government is making it harder to vote in the local elections

By Darren Hughes

When thousands of people go to vote in the local elections today, they will find that something has changed. In ten council areas, they'll need to bring ID to the polling station. Without it, they'll be turned away.

The government is once again piloting mandatory voter identification, following trials last year that saw 350 people denied the vote. Apparently it was not enough. This time, ten councils are taking part in the scheme.

Ministers are apparently intent on ploughing ahead. But make no mistake: this is a 'show your papers' policy. It presents a significant risk to democratic access and equality.

Prior to the 2018 pilots, an unprecedented coalition of over 40 leading civil society groups, charities and academics joined the Electoral Reform Society in opposing mandatory ID plans, including Age UK, Stonewall, Liberty, The Salvation Army, Migrants' Rights Network, the British Youth Council and the Race Equality Foundation. Those groups are still against proposals that could pull up the drawbridge for millions of potential voters.

And it is millions. Research by the Electoral Commission shows that around 3.5 million citizens – 7.5% of the electorate – do not have access to photo ID. If voter identification requirements were restricted solely to passports or driving licenses, around 11 million citizens – 24% of the electorate – could potentially be disenfranchised. Getting ID costs time and money, which many people don't have.

It's a dramatic shift in the burden in the burden of responsibility – away from police and returning officers to ordinary people.

You could justify such a shift if there was evidence of widespread fraud, but that evidence does not exist. New figures released by the Electoral Commission in March show that, of the 266 cases investigated by police relating to the 2018 local and mayoral elections and local by-elections, more than half (140) were campaigning offences, and just one in five (57) related to complaints made about the voting process.

Personation fraud at the polling station – the crime of pretending to be someone else at the ballot box, which is what the government's continuing voter ID pilots claim to address – accounted for just eight of the 266 allegations made in 2018. No further action was taken for seven of these allegations and one was locally resolved. That is the apparent crisis which this policy addresses.

And while the government fixes problems that do not exist, it ignores those that do. As we have consistently warned, our elections are wide open to foreign interference and meddling

That isn't from people wandering from polling station to polling station in trench coats, pretending to be other people. It's from our analogue-age campaign-funding rules and unregulated online political advertising.

Foreign states and unscrupulous campaigners will be pleased with this state of affairs, where the government makes it harder for people to vote, rather than take on big money in politics. But for everyone else, today's bureaucratic requirements at the polling station will be pointless and counter-productive.

2 May 2019

Elections in Britain: why you should not vote

Vote! That's what students in Britain are being told on election day. But here's an alternative view: Abstain and withhold your approval of a flawed system.

By Arsentiy Novak

It is a near impossible task to find a student who has not been pressured to vote in Britain's snap election today.

Widespread dissatisfaction – to use a gentle term – with Prime Minister Theresa May, with a lack of consistency in her Conservative Party's manifesto and with her inability to extinguish rising terrorist aggression sets young hearts ablaze. The majority of youngsters stand behind the meek and mild Jeremy Corbyn, leader of the UK Labour Party.

But no matter how Thursday's election ends, there is a deep and growing sense of unrest over an inconspicuous illusion: that the individual matters and that the election offers a genuine choice.

I want to present an alternative view.

'A vote by itself confers consent.'

Voting is a necessary part of any democracy and underpins our state. Voting keeps the wheels of democracy turning. But we, the voters, only make up the tractor's engine. The government is in the driver's seat, and propaganda is its fuel.

So what gives a government legitimacy? Quite simply, our consent. Before I turn to the notion of a vote, there is a proposition that must be rejected: That we offer our consent simply by acquiescing to an elected government. That we are free to leave the country if we don't like it, and we should accept this as fair.

This notion – that we are free to depart if we are not content – is undiluted masochism, and its proponents are sadistic. Their claim is this: I provide a life that I decide is best for you, and in return you repay me with your freedom and gratitude. Failing this, you will be punished. You must accept this bargain as well deserved and proper.

Well, I don't.

A vote by itself confers consent. It provides legitimacy to a system designed mainly to correct deviants – those who stray from the designated path. With our vote, we legitimise a system that works like a parasite, eating away at its creators and forcing us into a contract of coercion. We select our leaders, and so face the consequences.

'Abstaining from voting is one of the few liberties we can still enjoy.'

Slavery is often tempting to our species. We want a government that's strong and rigid to outside oppressors, and just and good to those within. May promises the former, Corbyn the latter. Whomever you 'choose', remember this: Tyranny takes root in the erosion of individuality. One is coerced into bowing to the wishes of the majority. A majority whose consciousness is formed by the government.

To simplify, let's substitute 'father' for 'government'. We are told that we are free because we can vote and therefore choose between options presented to us. These options are chosen by the father, put forward by the father, limited by the father, and our choice is influenced by the father.

Want to say this is not true? Want to say you are the one who makes the decisions? But who are you if not the consequence of your parentage? Our very way of thinking is moulded by our father. In Britain, we can choose how the father looks, but do you really think the choice is free?

Abstaining from voting is one of the few liberties we can still enjoy, something our friends in Argentina, Australia, Belgium, Brazil, Luxembourg and North Korea – where voting is compulsory – have lost. Use it.

If you question the legitimacy of state rule, voting is nonsensical. Abstain while you can, and you will still have a right to complain.

After all, you will have had nothing to do with the forthcoming circus.

8 June 2017

The people who can't vote in an election

By Heather Saul

The right to vote is a human right, right? Well, you might think so, but it's not that simple.

The right to free elections, which includes the right to vote, is protected under the Human Rights Act.

But that doesn't mean everyone living in the UK can vote in the general election today. The right to vote is not absolute, which means conditions can be imposed.

People who can't vote:

Anyone convicted of crime who is serving their sentence in prison

In March 2017, there were 74,623 people in prison banned from voting, regardless of the severity of their crime.

Men and women who are in prison on remand, so unconvicted and unsentenced prisoners and those awaiting trial, can vote.

Civil prisoners can also vote. Civil prisoners are people who are being detained but have not been convicted of a criminal offence, such as non-payment of a fine or contempt of court.

Members of the House of Lords

Members of the House of Lords cannot vote in a general election. However, they can vote in local authority elections and the European Parliament.

EU citizens who live in the UK but do not have British citizenship

EU citizens of the UK, Republic of Ireland, Cyprus and Malta who live in the UK can still vote.

Anyone found guilty of corruption or illegal practices in connection with an election

This applies to those found guilty within the previous five years.

Some victims of domestic violence

Victims of domestic violence living in refuges who can't provide evidence to prove they or someone in their household will be in danger if their name or address is published on the Electoral Register are not eligible to vote anonymously. This has prompted a campaign by women who say they are disenfranchised because voting without being anonymous would put them in danger.

People who are homeless can vote

People who have to sleep on the streets or have no fixed address can register using the address they spend the most time at. According to guidelines from Shelter, this could include a friend's house, a hostel or a day centre. There is advice on how to do that on the Shelter website.

8 June 2017

Should the voting age be lowered to 16?

By Barney Stephenson

In 1969, Harold Wilson's Labour government lowered the voting age from 21 to 18. Fifty years on, some believe the time has come to lower the voting age to 16.

The idea is not a new one. It was first rejected by Parliament back in 1999 and again in 2005.

But in 2014, 16- and 17-year-olds were granted a vote in Scotland's independence referendum.

This – combined with the overwhelming age gap between remain and leave voters in the UK's 2016 European referendum – has firmly placed the voting age back on the national agenda.

Who supports lowering the voting age?

Currently, all the opposition parties in Parliament back the idea of adding 1.5 million teenagers to the electorate by lowering the voting age to 16.

Labour leader Jeremy Corbyn stated: 'We cannot allow this Conservative government to deny one and a half million people their full rights as citizens.'

In 2017 a Bill brought by Labour MP Jim McMahon failed to go to a vote after running out of debating time despite the backing of the other opposition parties.

Politicians who advocate lowering the voting age often argue that at 16, citizens have taken on enough responsibilities to deserve the chance to have their say.

Molly Scott Cato, the Green Party's candidate for Bristol West, believes: 'At 16, you're eligible to pay taxes, you can leave home, you can get married, you can even join the armed forces.

'If you can do any of these things, you are entitled to vote – you are entitled to have a say in the direction of your country, you're entitled to have your say on the key issues affecting your life.'

Alternatively, Professor David Runciman says an ageing electorate means young people are now massively outnumbered resulting in an inbuilt bias against governments who plan for the future.

He goes several steps further than those advocating the vote at 16, suggesting the way to counter the democratic imbalance is to give the vote to everyone over the age of six.

Who opposes lowering the voting age?

Conservatives have countered advocacy of lowering the voting age by asserting that 18 is the age when somebody becomes recognised as an adult and full citizenship rights are obtained.

Questioned on the issue before to the last election, Theresa May said: 'I continue to think it's right for it to be 18.

'Of course we now expect young people to stay in educational training up until 18.'

Standing in for May at PMQs earlier this year, David Lidington, her de facto deputy, suggested that those under 18 did not have 'sufficient maturity and responsibility' to vote in elections.

This stance was labelled hypocritical and self-interested by Labour, who highlighted that Tories allow members aged 15, 16 and 17 to vote in their leadership elections.

Some consider support for votes at 16 to be a cynical ploy to introduce a demographic into the electorate that would be more likely to vote in favour of opposition parties.

Professor James Tilley agrees such decisions are made for political gain rather than from principled conviction. He posits that many of the responsibilities afforded to 16-year-olds are not as significant as those advocating votes at 16 make out.

For example, 16- and 17-year-olds must get permission from parents before they are able to marry or join the army.

He contests that rather than lowering the voting age it should be increased due to a slowing rate of maturity. He cites research by Prof. Lucinda Platt which shows that only 29% of 16- to 19-year-olds are currently in full-time work, compared to around four-fifths in the late '60s.

Yet, the largest obstacle for votes at 16 could simply be public opinion. In 2013, a YouGov poll showed that 60% of British adults opposed the idea and only 20% supported it.

YouGov research from 2018 shows that whilst the public are still opposed, there is growing support for extending the franchise, with the way in which the question is worded having a significant impact on the response. 34% of the public support 16- and 17-year-olds' *right* to vote, but only 24% backed *reducing* the voting age.

What would the impact be?

ONS research highlights that there are 88 out of 650 constituencies where the number of 16- and 17-year-olds outnumber the majority held by the sitting MP. 34 are held by Conservative MPs who are the most vulnerable to losing their seats should the franchise be extended – based on the notion that young people are more likely to vote Labour.

If these seats changed hands, Labour would become the largest party in Parliament.

It's possible lowering the vote could have had an equally substantial effect on the EU referendum. In a survey conducted by the Student Room 82% of 16- and 17-year-olds opted for remain. Such a turnout would have closed the gap of 1.2 million between Remain and Leave.

However, these predictions rely on all 16- and 17-year-olds turning out at the polls. But young people currently record the lowest levels of turnout, with 18-to-19-year-olds the age group least likely to vote at the 2017 general election.

The only other major European country to lower the voting age to 16 is Austria, in 2007. Prof. Sylvia Kritzinger says that the move hasn't particularly changed Austria's political landscape; however, it has resulted in more political education and therefore created habitual voters. Some 79% of Austrians aged 15 to 30 have voted in the last three years, the highest rate in Europe where the overall average is 64%.

Will it happen?

A change appears unlikely so long as the Conservatives remain in power.

However, with the rest of the major parties openly endorsing the idea and May's grip on power looking increasingly precarious it could be only a matter of time before the voting age is lowered to 16.

Who knows? Maybe in another 50 years, Prof. David Runciman's proposal of votes for six-year-olds will become a reality.

23 May 2019

Three good reasons the voting age should be raised to 21 – not cut to 16

By Tom Welsh

The prize for the most vacuous, the most cynical campaign in British politics today must surely go to those demanding that 16-year-olds be given the vote. No good reason is ever offered for doing so. Yes you can join the army or get married at 16, but only with parental permission. Elsewhere the trend is going in the other direction. I'm old enough to remember when the minimum age you could buy cigarettes was 16. You can't even leave full-time education now until 18.

Nevertheless, an unholy alliance of Remainers and the Left love the idea because they erroneously think it would give them a permanent electoral advantage. They look at the self-important children who played truant on Friday to shout anti-Tory slogans in London and are filled with hope, not despair. So they have given up trying to persuade actual voters and have elected to invent new ones. In the establishment's weird logic, at 16 you are not old enough to be judged responsible for becoming a jihadi bride in Syria, but quite capable of choosing who governs us.

Sorry, this won't do. If we were discussing this issue with any semblance of rationality, we would be debating raising the voting age, not cutting it. There are three arguments for doing so.

First is the issue of when we stop being children, and there is evidence that, developmentally at least, we now become adults at a later stage. In 2013, guidance for psychologists was updated to acknowledge that adolescence effectively ends at 25, not 18. A clinical psychologist told the BBC: 'We used to think that the brain was fully developed by very early teenagerhood and we now realise that the brain doesn't stop developing until the mid-20s or even early 30s.'

Second is the linked issue of when we start treating young people as adults. One explanation for why our brains might be developing less quickly is that there has been a cultural shift, wherein it is now perfectly acceptable socially to be dependent on parents or whoever for longer. The counter-argument is that it is harder for young people to be independent for economic reasons, like high housing costs. But that is beside the point: if you accept that the voting age is the societal consensus put into law of when we consider an individual to be fully adult, then it should be going up not down.

Third is the question of when younger people consider themselves to be adults. Many say they are grown up by 16, but that is not what they reveal through their actions. Teenage marriage rates have dropped dramatically, nearly half of young people won't enter full-time work until 21 because they are at university, and people are having children later.

Now, of course, I am not actually proposing increasing the voting age. Nothing could be better guaranteed to enrage a generation that already, and stupidly, considers their future to have been stolen by those older than them. But there is not an argument for votes at 16 that cannot be effectively countered by an argument for votes at 21. Restless youths should avoid opening this particular can of worms.

16 February 2019

Voting systems in the UK

The House of Commons, devolved assemblies and mayors in the UK are elected using different voting systems. The Commons and the House of Lords also use a variety of voting systems for internal elections.

Voting systems, also known as electoral systems, are the method by which we elect representatives. A voting system determines the rules on how parties and candidates are elected.

A number of different voting systems are used to elect mayors and representatives to the House of Commons, Scottish Parliament, National Assembly for Wales, Northern Ireland Assembly, European Parliament and UK local authorities.

First-past-the-post

First-past-the-post is used to elect MPs to the House of Commons and for local elections in England and Wales.

Under first-past-the-post, the UK or local authority is divided into numerous voting areas, i.e. constituencies or wards. At a general or local election, voters put a cross (X) next to their preferred candidate on a ballot paper.

Ballot papers are then counted and the candidate that has received the most votes is elected to represent the constituency or ward.

Alternative Vote (AV)

The Alternative Vote (AV) is used to elect the majority of chairs of select committees in the House of Commons. The AV is also used for the election of the Lord Speaker and by-elections for hereditary peers.

Under AV, voters rank candidates in order of preference by marking 1, 2, 3 and so on next to names of candidates on a ballot paper. A voter can rank as many or as few candidates as they like or just vote for one candidate.

Ballot papers are then counted by using the first preference votes (i.e. those with a number 1 marked next to their name). If a candidate receives more than 50 percent of the first preference votes then they are elected.

If no candidate reaches this 50 percent threshold, then the candidate with the fewest first preference votes is eliminated. Their second preference votes are then reallocated to the remaining candidates. If after this stage one candidate has more votes than the other remaining candidates put together, that candidate is elected.

If not, the process of elimination and reallocation of preference votes is repeated until one candidate has more

votes than the other remaining candidates put together, and is then elected.

Supplementary Vote (SV)

The Supplementary Vote (SV) system is used to elect the Mayor of London and other elected mayors in England and Wales.

The SV system is very similar to the AV system. Under SV, voters are limited to a first and second preference choice. A voter marks a cross in one column for their first preference candidate and another cross in a second column for their second preference (if they wish to do so).

The ballot papers are counted and if a candidate received more than 50 percent of the first preference votes on the first count, then they are elected.

If no candidate reaches the 50 percent threshold, the two candidates with the highest number of votes are retained and the other candidates are eliminated. The second preferences on the ballot papers of the eliminated candidates are counted and any cast for the two remaining candidates are transferred. The candidate with the most votes at the end of this process is elected.

Single Transferable Vote (STV)

The Single Transferable Vote system (STV) is used to elect the Deputy Speakers in the House of Commons. STV is also used for electing the Northern Ireland Assembly, local elections in Scotland and Northern Ireland and European Parliament elections in Northern Ireland.

Multi-member constituencies are required for STV which means constituencies are normally larger but elect several representatives rather than just one.

Under STV, voters rank candidates in order of preference by marking 1,2,3 and so on next to the names of candidates on a ballot paper. A voter can rank as many or as few candidates as they like or just vote for one candidate.

Each candidate needs a minimum number of votes to be elected. This number is calculated according to the number of seats and votes cast and is called a quota. The first preference votes for each candidate are added up and any candidate who has achieved this quota is elected.

If a candidate has more votes than are needed to fill the quota, that candidate's surplus votes are transferred to the remaining candidates. Votes that would have gone to the winner instead go to the second preference listed on those ballot papers.

If candidates do not meet the quota, the candidate with the fewest first preference votes is eliminated and the second preference votes are transferred to other candidates. These processes are repeated until all the seats are filled.

Additional Member System (AMS)

The Additional Member System (AMS) is used to elect the Scottish Parliament, the National Assembly for Wales and the London Assembly.

Under AMS, voters are given two votes; one for an individual candidate and one for a party. Individual candidates are elected to single-member constituencies using first-past-the-post (or the second ballot or alternative vote). Under the second, party vote, representatives (additional members) are elected proportionally to a larger region.

The percentage of votes obtained by the parties in the party vote (second ballot) determines the overall number of representatives including those elected for the single member constituencies after taking into account the seats gained in each region by each party in the first ballot.

Closed Party List

The Closed Party List system is used to elect Members of the European Parliament, with the exception of Northern Ireland which uses Single Transferable Vote.

A voter marks a cross on the ballot paper next to the party's name they wish to support. Once the ballot papers have been counted, each party gets the number of seats proportionate to the number of votes it has received in each constituency.

Multi-member constituencies are required for the Closed Party List which means constituencies are normally larger but elect several representatives rather than just one.

As voters choose parties rather than candidates, it is for the parties to determine the order in which candidates appear on the list and are then elected.

First past the post

First past the post is the name for the electoral system used to elect Members of Parliament (MPs) to Westminster.

What is first past the post?

Former British colonies tend to use the same voting system as Westminster. Many, including Australia, New Zealand, Ireland, Cyprus, Malta and South Africa have since stopped. But the US, Canada, India, and many Caribbean and African states still do.

How does first past the post voting work?

On election day, voters receive a ballot paper with a list of candidates. As only one MP will represent the area, each party only stands one candidate to choose from.

Voters usually put a cross next to their favourite candidate. But if they think their favourite has a low chance of winning, they may put a cross next to one they like with a better chance of winning.

'As there is only one candidate from each party, voters who support that party but don't like their candidate have to either vote for a party they don't support or a candidate they don't like'

How are first past the post votes counted?

During a General Election, 650 constituencies across the country each hold separate contests. To become an MP, a candidate needs the largest number of votes in their area. This means every MP has a different level of local support. In many areas, the majority of people will not have voted for their MP.

Even if millions of voters support the same party, if they are thinly spread out they may only get the largest number of votes in a couple of these contests. Tens of thousands of voters supporting the same party and living in the same area will end up with more MPs.

This means the number of MPs a party has in parliament rarely matches their popularity with the public.

'The number of MPs a party has in Westminster rarely reflects the number of votes the party's candidates received.'

Features and effects

This tends to generate two large parties, as small parties without a geographical base find it hard to win seats.

With a geographical base, parties that are small UK-wide can still do very well. This tends to mean that Westminster's electoral system benefits nationalist parties. For instance, half of Scottish voters voted for the SNP in 2015, but the SNP won 95 percent of Scotland's seats.

'First Past the Post tends to generate two large parties, as small parties without a geographical base find it hard to win seats.'

Westminster's First Past the Post voting system usually allows parties to form a government on their own. But, these governments may only have the support of 35 percent (Labour 2005), a record low, or 37 percent (Conservative 2015) of the country.

Westminster's voting system creates two sorts of areas. 'Safe seats', with such a low chance of changing hands that there is no point in campaigning, and 'swing seats', that could change hands.

As parties want to get as many MPs as possible, parties prioritise voters who might change their minds who live in swing seats. Parties design their manifestos to appeal to voters in swing seats, and spend the majority of their funds campaigning in them.

But, policies designed to appeal to voters in these seats may not help voters in the rest of the country. Voters who live in safe seats can feel ignored by politicians.

'Parties design their manifestos to appeal to voters in swing seats, and spend the majority of their funds campaigning in them.'

Constituency representation

Many swing seats have two candidates where either could get elected. But some have more. The more candidates with a chance of getting elected the fewer votes the winner needs. In 2015 a candidate won the Belfast South election with only 9,560 votes, or 24.5% of the total, a record low.

Under Westminster's First Past the Post system it is common for constituencies to elect MPs that more than half the voters didn't want.

To combat this, voters try to second-guess the results. If a voter thinks their favourite candidate can't win, they may vote for one with the best chance of stopping a candidate they dislike from winning.

In 2015, a candidate won the Belfast South election with only 9,560 votes, or 24.5% of the total, a record low.

Holding the government to account

As the number of MPs a party gets doesn't match their level of support with the public, it can be hard for the public to hold the government to account.

More people can vote for a party's candidates compared to the last election, but they can lose MPs. The reverse can also happen.

In 1951 and 1974, the party had the most MPs wasn't the party that got the most votes from the public.

In New Zealand, the Labour Party won more votes than the National Party in 1978 and 1981, but the National Party remained the largest party and formed the government on both occasions.

Can democracy vote itself out of existence?

An article from The Conversation.

By Manjeet Ramgotra, Senior Teaching Fellow in Politics and International Studies, SOAS, University of London

THE CONVERSATIO

L ook at the state of the world's democratic nations, and it is easy to see why so many are concerned for the future of democracy.

Leaders such as Recep Tayyip Erdoğan, Vladimir Putin and Hungary's Viktor Orbán have centralised political power by changing their countries' constitutions, silencing dissent and controlling the media. Since 2016's coup attempt in Turkey, Erdoğan's government has used the subsequent state of emergency to incarcerate thousands without trial. Opposition politicians, judges, journalists and academics have been thrown in jail – all following a successful referendum that saw the office of president shed many of the restraints of parliament. The recent presidential elections then returned Erdoğan to office, albeit with the slimmest of majorities.

Given this climate of fear and censorship, the people cannot be said to have voted freely. But the fact that they did vote raises a fundamental question: can an electorate vote democracy away?

The people have spoken ... sort of

First of all, there are important distinctions between general elections and constitutional referendums, and each comes with its own set of democratic dangers.

In Turkey and the UK, narrow referendum results have endorsed fundamental constitutional change. But these referendums are not, like general elections, exercising the democratic right to select leaders. Instead, they are making complex governmental decisions that often require understanding of specialist information, way beyond what could reasonably be expected of an ordinary person. Voting on such questions – usually concerning fundamental long-term change – ought to, and often does require a super majority. Otherwise, as we can see from the 52/48 split in the UK's Brexit vote, the results can be highly contentious.

General elections do not require super majorities, and the government is formed from whichever party captures enough seats to command the legislative assembly, or, in a proportional system, the opportunity to lead a coalition. Frequently, the popular vote is not reflected in the number of seats a party wins. In Hungary, Orbán's Fidesz party won 49% of the vote, but 133 of the 199 available seats. In the US, Hillary Clinton gained more votes overall, but lost the presidency under the electoral college system.

These divergences are well-established, and when elections are contested between two moderate parties trying to appeal to the middle ground (as has been the case across Europe for many years), such anomalies have not caused too much instability. But in today's more extreme, divergent political climate, a greater number of governments could emerge that are divisive and extremely unstable. When there is enough support for the extremes, they can be elected against the wishes of the majority of the population, leaving the ordinary voter faced with 'democratically elected' leaders whose policies they vehemently oppose.

Tale as old as time

The concept of electorate-mandated autocracy goes back as far as the modern democratic state. In his *Eighteenth Brumaire*, Karl Marx lamented the election of Napoleon III in 1848 that led to him declaring himself 'emperor' in 1852. Marx observed how easy it was for an already centralised power to centralise further, and remove the institutions that might stop it from doing so. He lamented too, how easy it was to adopt a 'heroic' personality, and to strategically appeal to the interests of specific groups of people in order to win an election. The appeals are of course hollow, but they can harness the support of those seduced by charisma and strength.

To suggest that electorates deliberately, or consciously vote for autocracy is another matter. The standard explanation is that people know not what they do – that they are swept up in a desire to be part of something greater than themselves. This is partly true, but there are certainly those that support autocracy and hold extreme views. When these elements represent a significant-enough minority they can sometimes sweep enough people into their narratives to elect an extreme leader whose views do not represent the body politic.

More than a vote

But even in a vote with high turnout, an electorate free of disproportionately powerful minorities, and a legislative assembly aligned entirely with the popular vote, the results of an election could be wholly undemocratic. An election, to hold validity, must be 'free and fair'.

Many recent votes have been blighted by constraints on the press, manipulation of social media and data (note the Cambridge Analytica story), and defamatory campaigns that have strangled the free flow of information. Targeted attacks on those representing 'the establishment' (such as George Soros during the Hungarian elections), destabilise the moderate views and institutions associated with them, and foster a divisive 'us and them' mentality.

The institutions that structure political power and authority can also easily be centralised, particularly in moments of recognised stress, such as war or a state of emergency. These provide a reason or excuse for consolidation of executive power, allowing the governing class to make decisions without having to go through regular legislative channels. And once in place, these can be difficult to reverse. Turkey's state of emergency, the US Patriot Act and Britain's Prevent legislation are all examples of the power states have acquired to act without regard for due process.

Turkey's presidential elections, and its presidential referendum, were not democratic because the state had already become autocratic. Rather, they were exercises in projecting an image of democracy, since states that run elections are popularly assumed to be democratic. In reality the vote was not free, so the people did not 'vote against' democracy.

Democracy is about more than just voting. It is about freedom of speech, the separation of executive from legislative power, judicial independence, and political equality. Democratic institutions exist to keep power from becoming centralised in a single, despotic location. Once these institutions begin to weaken, and the only remaining element of democracy is the pretence of elections, then democracy in its meaningful form is already gone.

Powerless votes perpetuating pre-existing autocracies are barely votes at all. And a democratic vote that votes against democracy, probably wasn't very democratic in the first place.

16 July 2018

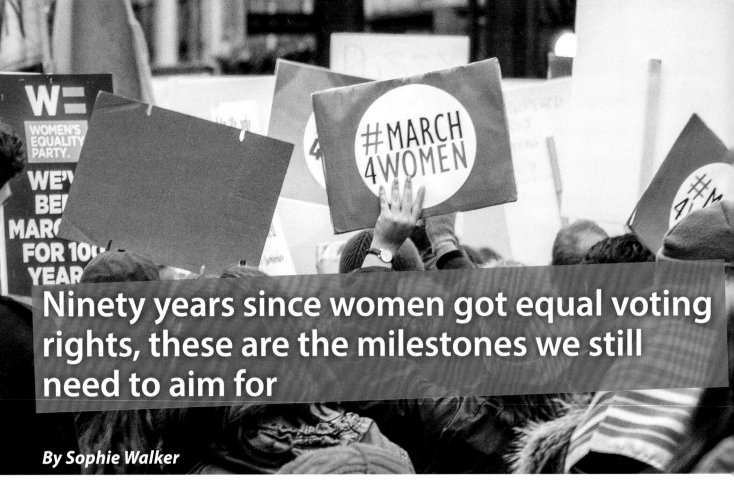

Ninety years since women got equal voting rights, these are the milestones we still need to aim for

By Sophie Walker

Today marks 90 years since women got equal voting rights to men. Given that this year we have focused on celebrating 100 years of suffrage to a first group of largely white and educated women, this alternative commemoration is a chance to remember that equal rights are not equal if some women must wait longer – and redouble our efforts on behalf of all.

The gap between partial and universal suffrage is an echo from the past that activists of today must heed. Because that gap is one into which too many women are still falling: working-class women, women of colour, disabled women, lesbian women, migrant women, refugee women.

I recently asked two women of colour what they thought of the women's movement today. One looked at me consideringly and said: 'Nothing. It's a Western concept for white women.' The other said: 'It makes me think of a rolling snow boulder – never going in a straight line but picking up bits and bobs along the way. Expanding, but never uniformly.'

I am driven to do better at lifting up all women

As the white, middle-class leader of the only feminist political party in Britain – working every day with an awareness that my whiteness and middle-classness only confirms for some women the failings of feminism – I am driven every day to do better at building a movement that lifts all women. Because not one of us can have equality until we all have it.

'Divide and rule is one of the most basic lessons in the art of war.'

This seems like a fairly straightforward principle to me, but every day I meet women and men who still believe that the women who have been flattened by centuries of legislative, economic and cultural oppression simply need to try harder. That women have choices within a system structured to make sure they have none.

Those with power will always try to split those who challenge their power – divide and rule is one of the most basic lessons in the art of war. Political parties address women's inequality through hashtag campaigns, piecemeal legislative tweaks, the occasional equality assessment long after the damage is done, then move along to the next thing, leaving the women in their parties to argue amongst themselves whether it's enough. CEOs make one female board appointment grudgingly, every ten years, as proof that only some women are capable or tough enough to make it in business – leaving it to their women's networks to debate how many more mentors and resilience-training programmes are required to help them endure sexist workplaces.

Feminism is not a hobby

And women seeking a different way are put up against other women seeking to survive by looking after themselves first. I've spent far too much of this centenary year invited to debate feminism as though it's all a bit silly. Questionable. A hobby for women who have never felt real hardship. I've been asked to defend a 'MeToo movement' depicted as hurting good men's reputations – never mind that not one Westminster MP has lost his job. I've been asked to defend pay gap reporting as though it's actually a cover for women making the wrong 'lifestyle choices' and 'wanting it all'.

> *'One hundred years later, while women may have the right to vote, no mainstream political party considers their needs and experiences equally to those of the men'*

I've also had moments of joy this Centenary celebrating the women who have closed the gap, from the original suffragists who did not give up until all women had the vote, to the women from across the political spectrum who are increasingly setting aside partisan differences to work together – a particular pleasure to Women's Equality Party members who often belong to WEP and another party owing to our affiliate membership scheme, designed to do just this – to the heroines of the women's sector who on dwindling funding nevertheless provide extraordinary levels of support to women at the very margins of our society.

I'm the leader of the Women's Equality Party – what I want couldn't be clearer

The more of us there are who call ourselves feminists, the more effective we will be at challenging the power of those who try to divide us. But that means the agenda for change has to be one from which we all benefit. Progress towards bodily autonomy is not progress unless and until Northern Irish women are freed from the draconian legislation that

every day forces them to travel to other parts of the UK to seek help. The new Domestic Violence Bill is not progress unless and until specialist services are properly funded to deliver support to the most marginalised women. Pay gap reporting is not progress unless and until companies are required to report on race and disability. Shared parental leave is not progress unless and until fathers are properly remunerated.

The ten-year gap between partial and universal suffrage was a deliberate decision by Parliamentarians to ensure at first that the number of women with voting rights was not greater than the number of men with voting rights. One hundred years later, while women may have the right to vote, no mainstream political party considers their needs and experiences equally to those of the men for whom our systems and institutions are designed. It's easier to set us to debating each other and suggesting we are confused in our own approaches to this. 'But what is it you want?' I am challenged, constantly. I'm the Leader of the Women's Equality Party – it couldn't be clearer.

When we stop to debate whether we need feminism, women fall through the gap

We don't have the time to debate whether we need feminism. Every time we stop to do so, more women fall into the gap between what has been achieved so far and what is yet to be done. Every time we debate childcare as a luxury, more women fall into the gap. Every time we debate sexual violence as hysteria, more women fall into the gap.

We have to fill the gap. We have to catch and lift up our sisters. For some women that means accepting challenges when we fail to see and understand multiple and intersecting layers of discrimination. For other women it means the far harder work of trusting people not to let you down. For leaders it means remembering that leadership is not a title but an act of solidarity. For activists it means remembering that a movement is supposed to do just that: move. Not stagnate.

So happy 90th anniversary to us. May all future milestones in the fight for women's equality be ones that we can all celebrate.

2 July 2018

Democracy in Retreat – *Freedom In The World 2019*

Challenges to American democracy are testing the stability of its constitutional system and threatening to undermine political rights and civil liberties worldwide.

Unpacking 13 years of decline

Freedom in the World has recorded global declines in political rights and civil liberties for an alarming 13 consecutive years, from 2005 to 2018. The global average score has declined each year, and countries with net score declines have consistently outnumbered those with net improvements.

♦ **A widespread problem:** The 13 years of decline have touched all parts of the world and affected Free, Partly Free, and Not Free countries alike. Every region except Asia-Pacific has a lower average score for 2018 than it did in 2005, and even Asia declined when countries with less than one million people–mostly small Pacific Island states–are excluded. Not Free countries as a group suffered a more significant score drop than Free or Partly Free countries, which also declined.

♦ **Faltering post–Cold War democratisation:** The end of the Cold War facilitated a wave of democratisation in the late 20th century, but a large share of countries that made progress during that time were unable to maintain it. On average, countries that earned a status upgrade–from Not Free to Partly Free, or Partly Free to Free–between 1988 and 2005 have faced an 11 percent drop in their numerical score during the 13 years of decline.

♦ **Consolidated democracies slip:** Social and economic changes related to globalization have contributed to a crisis of confidence in the political systems of long-standing democracies. The democratic erosion seen among Free countries is concentrated in consolidated democracies–those that were rated Free from 1985 through to 2005, the 20-year period before the 13-year decline.

Freedom in the World 2019

● Free ● Partly Free ● Not Free

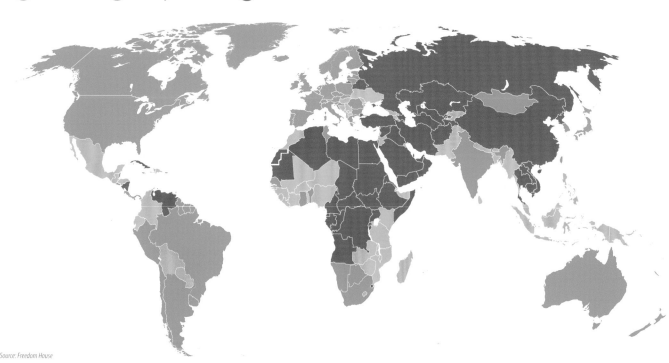

Source: Freedom House

Despite a continued downward trajectory overall, there were several more countries with net improvements in 2018 than in 2017, and a somewhat smaller number with net declines. This does not mean the threat to democracy is coming to an end. Hostile forces around the world continue to challenge the institutions meant to protect political rights and civil liberties, and the damage accrued over the past 13 years will not soon be undone.

Freedom in the World 2019 Freedom Status Changes

Hungary: Hungary's status declined from Free to Partly Free due to sustained attacks on the country's democratic institutions by Prime Minister Viktor Orbán's Fidesz party, which has used its parliamentary supermajority to impose restrictions on or assert control over the opposition, the media, religious groups, academia, NGOs, the courts, asylum seekers, and the private sector since 2010.

Serbia: Serbia's status declined from Free to Partly Free due to deterioration in the conduct of elections, continued attempts by the government and allied media outlets to undermine independent journalists through legal harassment and smear campaigns, and President Aleksandar Vučić's de facto accumulation of executive powers that conflict with his constitutional role.

Nicaragua: Nicaragua's status declined from Partly Free to Not Free due to authorities' brutal repression of an antigovernment protest movement, which has included the arrest and imprisonment of opposition figures, intimidation and attacks against religious leaders, and violence by state forces and allied armed groups that resulted in hundreds of deaths.

Uganda: Uganda's status declined from Partly Free to Not Free due to attempts by long-ruling president Yoweri Museveni's government to restrict free expression, including through surveillance of electronic communications and a regressive tax on social media use.

Zimbabwe: Zimbabwe's status improved from Not Free to Partly Free because the 2018 presidential election, though deeply flawed, granted a degree of legitimacy to the rule of President Emmerson Mnangagwa, who had taken power after the military forced his predecessor's resignation in 2017.

The United States in decline

Challenges to American democracy are testing the stability of its constitutional system and threatening to undermine political rights and civil liberties worldwide. As part of this year's report, Freedom House offers a special assessment of the state of democracy in the United States midway through the term of President Donald Trump. While democracy in America remains robust by global standards, it has weakened significantly over the past eight years, and the current president's ongoing attacks on the rule of law, fact-based journalism, and other principles and norms of democracy threaten further decline.

Having observed similar patterns in other nations where democracy was ultimately overtaken by authoritarianism, Freedom House warns that the resilience of US democratic institutions in the face of such an assault cannot be taken for granted.

Freedom House has tracked a slow overall decline in political rights and civil liberties in the United States for the past eight years, punctuated by an unusual three-point drop for developments in 2017. Prominent concerns have included Russian interference in US elections, domestic attempts to manipulate the electoral system, executive and legislative dysfunction, conflicts of interest and lack of transparency, and pressure on judicial independence and the rule of law.

This year, the United States' total score on the 100-point scale used by *Freedom in the World* remains the same as in the report covering 2017, with two indicators changing in opposite directions:

◆ The score for freedom of assembly improved, as there was no repetition of the protest-related violence that had led to a lower score for the previous two years. In fact, there was an upsurge of civic action and demonstrations on issues ranging from women's rights and immigration policy to the problem of mass shootings in schools.

◆ The score for equal treatment before the law declined due to government policies and actions that improperly restricted the legal rights of asylum seekers, signs of discrimination in the acceptance of refugees for resettlement, and excessively harsh or haphazard immigration enforcement policies that resulted in the separation of children from adult family members, among other problematic outcomes.

The United States currently receives a score of 86 out of 100 points. While this places it below other major democracies such as France, Germany, and the United Kingdom, it is still firmly in the Free category. Nevertheless, its decline of eight points in as many years is significant. The United States' closest peers with respect to total *Freedom in the World* scores are Belize, Croatia, Greece, Latvia, and Mongolia.

5 February 2019

Ranked and mapped: which countries have the most women in parliament

Women worldwide hold less than a quarter of seats in parliaments and senates.

By Odette Chalaby

Half of the world's population are women, but today women only hold 23% of all seats in parliaments and senates globally. And the most recent world rankings from the Inter-Parliamentary Union show that the countries doing well are not the ones you might expect.

Many of the big Western-style democracies are nowhere near the top. The UK currently ranks number 39 in the world with less than a third of the Houses of Commons and Lords being women. Australia is ranked 49 and Canada is ranked 62, both with just more than a quarter of female parliamentarians. The US ranks all the way down at 98; less than one in five seats in Congress are currently taken by women.

Yet some of the data is much more promising – and surprising. In the world's top two countries for female representation, Rwanda and Bolivia, women now make up parliamentary majorities.

While numbers of women are increasing overall – in 2000, women took a world average of only 13.8% of seats across both houses, 10% less than today – the pace of change is slow. At the current rate, 50:50 parity will not be reached for another 50 years.

Rwanda is number one

In every year since 2004, Rwanda has had more women in parliament than any other country around the world. For the last four years, it has had a record 64% of its lower house made up of women.

The roots of its high figures can be traced back to the devastating genocide of 1994. An estimated 800,000 Rwandans were slaughtered within 100 days, with the killings and exodus cutting the population by about a third.

Many men in particular were killed or forced to flee, and records show that immediately after the genocide, women astonishingly made up about 70% of the remaining population. Most of these women had not been educated and few expected to have a career outside the home, but the traumatic effects of the massacre changed things substantially.

President Kagame decided women's labour would be needed to rebuild the shattered country, and promoted many top-down equality initiatives to that effect. As part of his efforts, the constitution of 2003 decreed that women should make up 30% 'of posts in decision-making organs', including the lower and upper legislative houses.

In the House of Deputies, 24 of 80 seats have since been reserved for women. But in that first election, already women won significantly more than their assigned minimum, taking almost half of all seats. This represented a leap in women's political representation of almost 20% in one year.

Strikingly, around a third of the top 30 countries in the global rankings are post-conflict states, including Angola, Uganda, Burundi, and Nicaragua. Parallels could be drawn with the stark leaps in gender equality experienced in Europe after both world wars. In the UK, women won the vote in 1918 having carried out 'men's' jobs during the First World War.

Latin American countries jump up the rankings

Despite Latin America's high rates of violence and machismo – it is home to some of the world's highest rates of female murders and less than half of its female population earns an income – it has taken giant strides in the direction of equality in political representation.

This year, of the top ten countries around the world for women's representation in parliament, four are from Latin America (Bolivia #2, Cuba #3, Nicaragua #5, Mexico #7).

As a region, the Americas have witnessed the greatest aggregate changes in this regard over the past 20 years. While in 2000 the region had an average of only 15% of women in the upper and lower legislative houses, today it is the second best in the world with almost one in three legislators being women. In recent years, Latin America has also had more female presidents than any other part of the world, although Chile's Michelle Bachelet is currently the only one.

These parliamentary gains have followed widespread introduction of gender quotas from the late 1990s onwards. Gender quotas for elected office have now been adopted by 16 Latin American countries, and most are mandated by law, requiring political parties to nominate a minimum percentage of female candidates.

Argentina was a pioneer, being the first in the region to adopt quotas in 1991. It was also the first with a female president – Isabel Péron was elected in 1974.

Yet, it is Bolivia that truly stands out for its impressive leaps in women's representation. While in 2000 only 12% of Bolivia's parliamentary seats were held by women, today women make up the majority, holding 53%. Quotas here have played a clear role. Since constitutional changes in

Women in senates 2017

% of women in senates

0%   50%

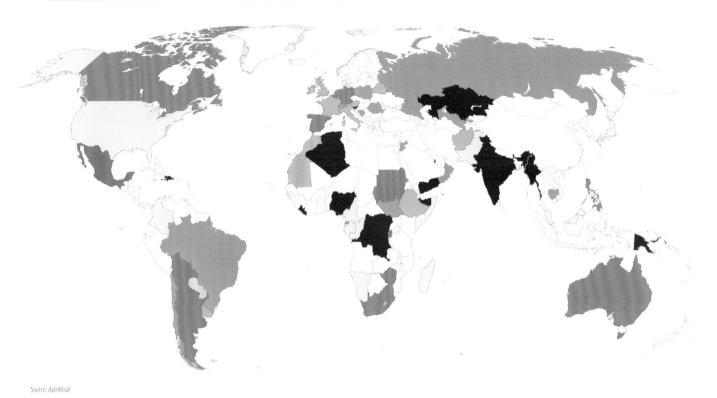

Source: Apolitical

2010, Bolivian women must occupy at least half of all elected government positions. To ensure this parity, candidate lists must be drawn up by alternating between women and men; the 'zipper' system.

Nordic region still at the top

Despite these impressive leaps, no region has touched the overall dominance of the Nordic countries. Since the year 2000, the region has consistently had an average of around two-fifths of its legislators being women.

Yet women's political representation is no longer rising so rapidly. In fact, Norway, Sweden, and Denmark have seen little change at all over the past two decades.

Unlike in Latin America, few countries in the region have mandatory gender quotas. Instead, women's more equal representation can be attributed to broader levels of gender equality across society. The top four in the World Economic Forum's latest *Global Gender Gap Report*, a ranking of countries on a wide range of gender equality measures, are Iceland, Finland, Norway and Sweden.

Higher equality in the region stems from decades of reform. Strong child care provisions, flexible working options for parents, and lengthy paternity leave offerings have led to very high female labour force participation and allowed more women to rise to positions of leadership. While there

may not be mandatory quotas for politics, Norway has also been the first of several countries in the region to implement gender quotas for private sector leadership; since 2008, publicly listed companies have been required to have 40% of each sex on their boards.

A look to the future

While this data shows that the world is making progress on women's representation, much remains to be done. Quotas, as in South America, are a controversial but often successful short-term mechanism to involve more women in the political sphere. But there are many other routes to improve political inclusiveness, as Scandinavia shows. Making the political workplace more welcoming, curbing intimidation and violence towards female politicians, and providing more arenas for women to meet and network are just some policies governments could use.

What is clear is that unless politics becomes more attractive to and accepting of women, half the world's population will remain half-represented for years to come.

19 September 2017

Women's votes: six amazing facts from around the world

An article from The Conversation

THE CONVERSATION

By Rebecca Wright, Barrister and Human Rights Lecturer, Sheffield Hallam University

On 6th February 1918, British women – (well, the wealthy ones over 30) – were given the right to vote. And since the 1960s, women have been voting in British national elections at basically the same rate as men. But how is the rest of the world doing? Here's a snapshot.

1. Ecuador: transgender friendly (at voting booths)

In Ecuador, men and women vote separately. The country was in the headlines last year when it decided to allow transgender people to choose the male or female line, according to the gender with which they identify. Diane Rodriguez, a transgender woman, described the harassment she would face in the male line and her relief that she could now vote without discrimination.

2. Vatican City: only place women can't vote

The only election held in Vatican City is when cardinals vote for a new pope. Women cannot be cardinals (despite the hope a few years ago that Pope Francis might appoint female cardinals) and so this is an exclusively male electorate.

That said, the majority of Vatican City's approximately 800 residents, including men, are excluded from this vote.

3. Saudi Arabia: latest place to let women vote

Saudi Arabia is the most recent country to grant women the vote. In 2015, they were given the right to take part in municipal elections.

Although this marked significant progress for Saudi women, a system of male guardianship makes it difficult in practice for women to vote. Saudi women are unable to drive themselves to the polling booths (though from June 2018 women will be granted driving permits). It's therefore no surprise that less than 10% of Saudi's voters in the 2015 elections were women.

4. Pakistan: one of the biggest gender gaps

Female participation in Pakistani elections is among the lowest in the world. Statistics from Pakistan's 2013 elections showed that turnout for women voters was less than 10% in nearly 800 polling stations. In some areas, female voter turnout was as low as 3%. Although Pakistani women were given the vote in 1956, community and religious leaders in some of the most conservative parts of the country prevent women from voting.

Leaflets were circulated in the 2013 elections warning men not to allow female family members to vote because it was 'un-Islamic.' These practices continued in 2015 local elections.

5. Sexual violence against women on the rise

Human Rights Watch published a report in 2017 which documented the sexual violence against women in Kenya's 2017 elections. These incidents were unfortunately representative of a growing rise in violence against women in elections. A recent United Nations report documents how women are increasingly victims of politically motivated rape and other forms of sexual violence, preventing them from participating freely in elections.

6. China: women voters vastly outnumbered by men

In 2017, more than 2,000 delegates attended the 19th Congress of the Communist Party of China in order to plan a five-year strategy. These powerful delegates were elected but only Party members were able to vote – and 74% of those members are male.

Despite the gender imbalance, that means that nearly 23 million women voters participated. The voter turnout among Party members was a staggering 99.2%. By comparison, the turnout for the British 2017 General Election was a measly 68.7%, with slightly more women voting than men.

A century on from votes for British women, progress has clearly been made around the world. The majority of the sexist laws that prevented women from voting have been repealed. However, there are still significant practical or cultural barriers that prevent female electoral participation.

Multiple international initiatives, including the United Nations programme on women's political participation, focus on removing barriers so women can vote. Such barriers are complex and multidimensional but include illiteracy (nearly two-thirds of the world's illiterate adults are women) and childcare responsibilities which prevent women from leaving the home. Much more needs to be done before every woman can have a meaningful say about the way their nation is run.

5 February 2018

What type of government does the United States have?

The United States government is composed of the legislative, the executive, and the judicial.

The US is a republic composed of 50 states, a number of territories, and a district, Washington D.C., which is also the country's capital city. The United States was formerly a British Colony and fully acquired its independence from Britain in 1776. After its independence, the US set out to acquire new territories, some of which were later admitted as states. The government of the United States is quite unique when compared to the government systems of other countries. Several nations tend to model their government around that of the US.

Government and Politics

The politics of the US takes place mainly under a two-party system. Two major political parties, the Democratic and Republican parties, dominate the political scene of the US. The presidency usually alternates between the two political parties. However, there are other minority political parties. The minority parties are rarely given recognition. In very rare instances do the minority parties form the government.

Federal Government

The president is the head of the federal government of the United States. However, each state forms its government for administration purposes. The powers of the state governments are exercised within restricted state boundaries. The most powerful figures in the states are the governors. The federal government of the US has three branches: the executive, the legislature, and the judiciary. The powers, roles, and limitations of the three branches are highlighted in the US constitution. The three branches of the government are as discussed below.

The executive

The head of the executive branch of the federal government is the president. The president is the most powerful figure in the government. She or he is both the head of the government and state. The president is assisted by the vice president who is elected as the running mate in a general election. The powers and functions of the president are, however, limited by the constitution. The responsibilities of the president include commander-in-chief of the armed forces and appointment of the members of the cabinet. The president is limited to a maximum of two terms of four years each.

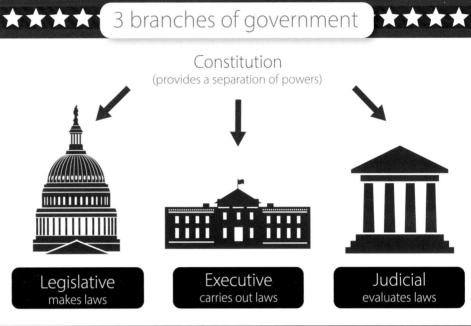

3 branches of government

Constitution
(provides a separation of powers)

| Legislative | Executive | Judicial |
| makes laws | carries out laws | evaluates laws |

The legislative

The legislative branch is composed of the two parliamentary houses. The parliament of the United States is bicameral, the Senate and the House of Representatives. The House of Representatives is composed of 435 members with each member representing a congressional district. The state with the highest population has the highest number of representatives. The delegates representing the territories of the US are also members of the House of Representatives.

The Senate is composed of 100 members. Each of the 50 states elect two members to the Senate regardless of the geographical size or population. The senators are elected after every six years. Senate approves the president's appointees by ensuring that the appointees are eligible to hold the office.

The judiciary

The judiciary of the United States is independent of influences from the Legislature and the Executive. It is made up of the Supreme Court, federal courts, other minority courts, and the organisations that support them. The judiciary is responsible for upholding, explaining, and applying laws. It is also responsible for hearing of cases and making legal decisions.

20 February 2018

United but different: differences and similarities between the US and the UK

By Olta Totoni

The Western democracies are the essential references for those countries and states that are in their beginnings. Countries like the United Kingdom and the United States of America with consolidated democracies make the difference and they also intertwine the old with the modern. The United States of America, a state of immigrants, a mosaic where every piece represents a certain state in comparison with The United Kingdom, a monarchy where the monarch gives her royal consent for economical and political facts.

The influence of the United Kingdom has been apparent throughout the history of the United States of America. From the colonies till now the situations have changed. They are two separate countries that collaborate freely with each other and offer equal chances for the relevant citizens.

Why is the United States of America considered to be a point of reference for all the western democracies? This federal state offers equal opportunity and it is characterised by freedom. Americans learn about the political system at an earlier age. The children learn how to vote, to elect the committees, to make a campaign etc. The voting process, the notion of the responsibility, the idea of the minority and majority are familiar for all the American citizens. The heart of the American democracy is the transparency and it is manifested in different aspects.

First, the American citizens have the right to participate in different meetings. As Americans they have the right to express their thoughts freely. They have their freedom of speech.

Second, the American citizens have the right to express their point of view by sending letters or electronic mails. The law for the freedom of the information has helped the American citizens to use public documents in order to understand better different situations, historical facts, etc. The face of America is changing quickly. What in the United Europe can be seen as a theory, in the United States it is considered to be practice. The power in the United States is well organised and this is done in order not to gain terrain and misuse the role. (Checks and Balances).

On the other hand, why is the United Kingdom considered to be a point of reference for all the western democracies? The United Kingdom is a parliamentary democracy. It is a constitutional monarchy. The Sovereign is the head of the country and the government. There is no written constitution in comparison with the United States where the constitution is the 'supreme law in the country'. In her role as a monarch the Queen is the head of the executive power and plays an integral role in the legislation. The Parliament has deep roots in the history of the United Kingdom. The medieval kings had to provide amounts of money for the public and private expenditure. If there were a need for extra resources, the Sovereign needed help from the barons in meetings which

CHECKS AND BALANCES

TRADITION AND INHERITANCE.

were handled several times in a year. During the thirteenth century the English kings had not enough income for their expenditure. They invited the barons, the representatives of the villages and towns in order to tax the additional taxes. This council included those representatives which were gathered on the basis of their title and that was later divided into two parts The House of Commons and The House of Lords.

The titles of the Crown derive partially from the Statute and partially from the descendants. The inheritance of the titles has been from one to another generation starting from the sons of the Sovereign that inherit the throne. When a daughter reigns she becomes a queen and she has equal rights with a king.

What is the role of the Monarchy in the United Kingdom?

The role of the Monarchy is very important. Throughout the years the British people have had second thoughts to keep the monarchy or not but they unanimously have voted for keeping it as a form of government. The role of the Queen is also very important. She has an important duty connected with the House of Commons and the House of Lords. Her role is preserved based on tradition and inheritance. The access of the public during the work of the two houses is an essential factor. The work of the two Houses is broadcasted on TV, on the radio and on the Internet in a registered form. The official reports are published daily in relevant websites. This way shows how much these democracies are developed.

Totally different is the model that the United States offers because the government of the United States is that 'of the people, by the people, for the people …'

The United Kingdom and the United States of America are two democracies that despite being the same in their values and principles, their differences are visible and this does not have to do only with their geographic aspects.

First, The United States of America is a democracy based on the President where the United Kingdom is based on the Prime Minister. Throughout history the United States of America was governed by different presidents. Most of them have been military men. They were elected through the free will of the people and through the most democratic principles. The United Kingdom follows a tradition of kings and queens that through wars and battles have created a strong nation with strong roots and with an important position in the international arena. Either the United Kingdom or the United States of America have diplomatic, cultural, economic and political relations.

Second, the governmental structure in the United Kingdom includes many traditions whereas the American system is flexible. For example, the election period of the President of the United States is scheduled up to four years. In the United Kingdom the Prime Minister can call a general election at any time within the five years.

Third, the United States is the first economy in the world. It is in an economical 'fight' with China of 'Who will be the next Super Power?' The United Kingdom is the fifth economy in the world but, it still remains one of the most industrialised countries in the world.

Fourth, the resign of the President can cause early elections or the vice president technically can take his office. In the United Kingdom, The Queen can elect the person she thinks is appropriate for the position. For example, Winston Churchill was appointed by the Queen during the World War II.

These states offer the best models of democracy in the world. Despite the governmental systems (The United States a federal state and the UK a monarchy) these two democracies are a good example of the freedom and rights of the people.

4 August 2017

The world's 6 most well-governed countries. Denmark, New Zealand, Canada, and Japan top 2018 BBC ranking

By Dr Amarendra Bhushan Dhiraj

I t turns out, Scandinavia's southernmost nation Denmark is the most well-governed country on Earth, according to a new analysis by the BBC. Regrettably, the United States is not to be found on this list…

Denmark's national parliament is called the Folketing, which translates as 'the people's thing'.

Perhaps unsurprisingly, New Zealand, the island nation in the Pacific Ocean ranked number 2 on the list, followed by Canada (No. 3), Japan (No. 4), Chile (No. 5), and Botswana (No. 6).

A massive study that ranks the world's most well-governed countries looked at data from the studies of various global organisations that try to measure how strictly a state adheres to the rule of law; how much trust its government inspires in its citizens; and how much social progress is in evidence.

The six best-governed countries in the world:

1. Denmark – The Nordic island nation tops the 2018 BBC ranking.

2. New Zealand – At number two, New Zealand has generous policies that support single parents, children, students, and seniors.

3. Canada – The country in the northern half of North America makes the list, while its neighbour the United States does not. Prime Minister Justin Trudeau currently leads Canada.

4. Japan – The only Asian country to make it into the top six most well-governed nations in the world. It functions under a constitutional monarchy where the Emperor serves mainly ceremonial duties.

5. Chile – Although it went through some serious political turmoil in decades past – now has 'one of South America's most stable and corruption-free governments'. It has affordable health care, high-quality infrastructure, and it's easy for foreigners to purchase property or start businesses there.

6. Botswana – Located in the heart of southern Africa, the country brings in significant revenues from diamond mining, the BBC said, and instead of benefiting only a wealthy elite, that money 'has been fairly well distributed throughout the country'. I never really knew this about Botswana, so now I'm intrigued and look forward to visiting one day.

16 January 2018

Key facts

- Parliament is formed of three main bodies. It is bicameral, which means that it has two houses in its seat in Westminster – the House of Commons and the House of Lords. The third body is its head – the Sovereign. (page 4)

- The House of Commons consists of 650 elected MPs. (page 4)

- We are one of only five countries in the world with uncodified constitutions – keeping company with Canada, Saudi Arabia, New Zealand and Israel. (page 4)

- In the UK, devolution means the transfer of power and decision making from the UK parliament in London to the assemblies in the respective countries. (page 9)

- With nearly 800 peers, the House of Lords is the world's second-largest decision-making body after China's National People's Congress. (page 11)

- Without the presence of the mace in the chamber, Parliament cannot lawfully meet, debate or pass laws. This rule dates back to the 17th century. (page 12)

- In 1432, Henry VI passed statutes declaring who was eligible to vote (male owners of land worth at least 40 shillings, or a freehold property – perhaps half a million people nationwide). (page 14)

- In 1893, New Zealand became the first self-governing country to allow women to vote. (page 15)

- The first woman elected to Parliament was Nancy Astor in 1918. (page 15)

- Since compulsory voting was introduced to Australia in 1924, turnout has never dropped below 91 percent. (page 16)

- In the 2017 General Election there were 22 million wasted votes – or 68% of the total. (page 16)

- Australia is one of only 19 countries out of 166 electoral democracies to make voting compulsory, and is the only English-speaking country to do so. (page 17)

- Research by the Electoral Commission shows that around 3.5 million citizens – 7.5% of the electorate – do not have access to photo ID. (page 18)

- In Argentina, Australia, Belgium, Brazil, Luxembourg and North Korea voting is compulsory. (page 19)

- In March 2017, there were 74,623 people in prison banned from voting, regardless of the severity of their crime. (page 20)

- In 1969, Harold Wilson's Labour government lowered the voting age from 21 to 18. (page 21)

- In 2014, 16- and 17-year-olds were granted a vote in Scotland's independence referendum. (page 21)

- 34% of the public support 16- and 17-year-olds' right to vote, but only 24% backed reducing the voting age. (page 22)

- First-past-the-post is used to elect MPs to the House of Commons and for local elections in England and Wales. (page 24)

- *Freedom in the World* has recorded global declines in political rights and civil liberties for an alarming 13 consecutive years, from 2005 to 2018. (page 32)

- Every region except Asia-Pacific has a lower average score for 2018 than it did in 2005. (page 32)

- Half of the world's population are women, but today women only hold 23% of all seats in parliaments and senates globally. (page 34)

- The UK currently ranks number 39 in the world with less than a third of the Houses of Commons and Lords being women. (page 34)

- Australia is ranked 49 and Canada is ranked 62, both with just more than a quarter of female parliamentarians. (page 34)

- In 2000 women took a world average of only 13.8% of seats across both houses, 10% less than today. (page 34)

- Since 2004, Rwanda has had more women in parliament than any other country around the world. (page 34)

- Argentina was a pioneer in introducing gender quotas. It was the first with a female president – Isabel Péron was elected in 1974. (page 34)

- On 6th February 1918, British women – (well, the wealthy ones over 30) – were given the right to vote. (page 36)

- Saudi Arabia is the most recent country to grant women the vote. In 2015, they were given the right to take part in municipal elections. (page 36)

Acts of Parliament

An Act of Parliament (also called a statute) is a law made by the UK Parliament.

All-party parliamentary groups (APPGs)

All-Party Parliamentary Groups (APPGs) are informal, cross-party groups formed by MPs and Members of the House of Lords who share a common interest in a particular policy area, region or country.

While they are not official parliamentary committees these groups can sometimes be influential because of their non-partisan, bicameral approach to an issue.

Backbench (backbenchers)

Backbenchers are MPs or members of the House of Lords that are neither government ministers nor opposition Shadow spokespeople. They are so called because, in the Chamber, they sit in the rows of benches behind their parties' spokespeople who are known as frontbenchers.

Bills

A bill is a proposal for a new law, or a proposal to significantly change an existing law, it may start in either the Commons or the Lords and must pass a series of stages in each House. Once the bill has been agreed by both Houses, it receives Royal Assent and becomes an Act of Parliament.

Budget (Finance Bill)

The Budget is the statement delivered to the House of Commons each year by the Chancellor of the Exchequer which sets out the state of the nation's finances and any planned changes to taxation and spending.

Coalition government

A coalition government is a government formed jointly by more than one political party. Parties may decide to form a coalition government if there is a hung parliament where no single party has a clear working majority in the House of Commons following a General Election.

Constituencies (Constituents)

A constituency is the specific geographical area that is represented by each MP in the House of Commons.

People who live in an MP's constituency are known as their constituents.

Constitution

A constitution is the set of principles and rules by which a country is organised and it is usually contained in one document.

Devolution

Devolution is the decentralisation of governmental power. Examples of devolution are the powers granted to the Scottish Parliament, the National Assembly for Wales, the Northern Ireland Assembly and to the Greater London and Local Authorities.

First Past the Post

First-past-the-post is a type of electoral system. In the UK it is the system used for the election of MPs to the House of Commons and for some local government elections.

Frontbench (frontbenchers)

A frontbencher is either a Government minister or an Opposition shadow spokesperson.

General elections

A general election is when the voters of the country cast their votes to elect Members of Parliament (MPs) to the House of Commons.

Government

The Government runs the country and has responsibility for developing and implementing policy and for drafting laws. Government departments and their agencies are responsible for putting government policy into practice.

Mace (The)

The mace in Parliament is the symbol of royal authority and without it neither House can meet or pass laws.

Motions

A motion is a proposal put forward for debate or decision in the House of Commons or House of Lords. A motion must be proposed (moved) before any debate or vote can take place in Parliament.

Manifesto

A manifesto is a publication issued by a political party before a general election. It contains the set of policies that the party stands for and would wish to implement if elected to govern.

Members of Parliament (MP)

A Member of Parliament is the person elected by all those who live in a particular area (constituency) to represent them in the House of Commons.

Opposition (The)

The Opposition, formally known as HM Official Opposition, refers to the largest political party in the House of Commons that is not in government.

Parliament

The United Kingdom Parliament is made up of three parts – the Crown, the House of Lords and the House of Commons. A Parliament is also the period of parliamentary time between one general election and the next.

Proportional representation

Proportional representation is an electoral system in which the distribution of seats corresponds closely with the proportion of the total votes cast for each party.

Royal Assent

Royal Assent is the Monarch's agreement that is required to make a Bill into an Act of Parliament.

Statute

A statute is an Act of Parliament: a law.

Activities

Brainstorming

◆ In small groups, discuss what you know about how government works. Consider the following points:

    • What is the constitution?

    • How do elections work?

    • What is the difference between the government and parliament?

◆ Create a mindmap with all that you know about the government in the UK

Research

◆ Create a questionnaire to find out people's views on lowering the voting age to 16. Is there a difference in opinions between different age groups?

◆ Read the article on page 24 'Voting systems in the UK' and research voting systems further.

◆ Choose a country and research further on when women were allowed to vote.

◆ Choose a country from the map on page 32, and do some research on whether they have a free democracy or not. Write some notes on your findings.

◆ Choose a government system from the article 'Democracy, monarchy and dictatorship: types of government systems' on page 1. Do some further research on countries that have this type of government.

Design

◆ Design a poster to promote young people to vote in an election.

◆ Choose one of the articles in this book and create an illustration to highlight the key themes/message of your chosen article.

◆ Design a leaflet on how the first past the post voting system works.

◆ Design a poster on promoting raising the voting age to 21.

◆ Using the time-line on pages 14–15 create your own time-line and add other dates that you think are important, such as when voting rights were improved.

Oral

◆ 'The voting age should be lowered to 16' Debate this motion as a class, with one group arguing in favour and the other against.

◆ As a class, discuss suffrage. How much do you know about women's rights in voting? Do you think that suffrage is universal? Should everyone be allowed to vote?

◆ In small groups, discuss whether you think compulsory voting is a good idea, or not.

◆ Read the article 'Elections in Britain: why you should not vote' on page 19 and discuss the author's point of view.

Reading/Writing

◆ Write an article exploring the different government types around the world.

◆ Write a one-paragraph definition of parliament.

◆ Imagine you work for a charity that promotes changing the voting system in general elections in the UK. Plan a social media marketing campaign that will raise awareness of the new system and to gain support.

◆ Write a diary entry of a woman in a country where it is hard to vote. Explain why you want to vote and the obstacles that are preventing you from doing so.

◆ Read one of the articles in the book and write five key points that stand out.

A
abstaining 19
Acts of Parliament 3, 6–8, 41
Additional Member System (AMS) 25
All-Party Parliamentary Groups (APPGs)
    41
Alternative Vote (AV) 24–5
Aristotle 1
Australia, compulsory voting 17

B
backbenchers 41
Bercow, John 10
Bill of Rights 14
Bills 6–8, 41
Botswana 39
Brexit 10, 11, 28
Budget (Finance Bill) 41

C
Cabinet 2
Canada 39
ceremonial mace 12–13
Charity Commission 2
Chile 39
China 36
Civil Service 3
Closed Party List 25
communism 1
compulsory voting 16–17
Conservative Party 21–2
    peers 11
constitutional monarchy 1
constitutional law 4
Corbyn, Jeremy 19, 21

D
Davison, Emily 15
debating 10
democracy 1, 28–9, 32
Denmark 39
Department for Work and Pensions 2
devolved governments 2, 3, 4, 9
dictatorships 1
draft legislation 3, 6

E
Ecuador 36
elections
    abstaining from voting 19
    compulsory voting 16–17
    first-past-the-post 9, 24, 26–7
    general 41
    local 18
    mandatory voter identification 18
    manifesto 41
    right to vote 20
    voting systems 24–5
Electoral Register, and right to vote 20
European Parliament 25
European Union 4
executive agencies 2

F
feminism, and politics 30–1
first-past-the-post 9, 24, 26–7
Freedom in the World 2019 32–3
frontbenchers 41

G
gender
    imbalance in voting 36
    see also women
general elections 41
government
    Cabinet 2
    Civil Service 3
    definition 41
    departments 2
    executive agencies 2
    how it works 2–3
    local 3, 18
    ministers 2, 4
    non-departmental public bodies
        (NDPBs) 2
    spending 4
    types of 1
    see also devolved government;
        legislation; Parliament
Government of Wales Act 1998 9
Green Papers 6
Green Party 21

H
hereditary peers 4, 11
Her Majesty's Inspectorate of Prisons 2
homelessness, and right to vote 20
House of Commons 2, 4–7, 10, 12–14
House of Lords 2, 4–7, 11
Human Rights Watch, on violence
    against women 36
Hungary 33

I
independent monitoring boards 2
Industrial Revolution 15

J
Japan 39
Johnson, Boris 11
Joint Committee on Statutory
    Instruments (JCSI) 8

L
Labour Party 21–2
    peers 11
Latin America, women's political
    representation 34–5
legislation 3
    Bills 6–8, 41
    constitutional law 4
    Green Papers 6
    Money Bills 8
    new laws 6–7
    Parliament's role 6
    secondary 8
    Statutory Instruments (SIs) 8

White Papers 6
Liberal Democrat Party, peers 11
local government 3, 18
London Assembly 25

M
mace, ceremonial 12–13
Magna Carta 4, 14
mandatory voter identification 18
manifesto 41
Marx, Karl 29
May, Theresa 19, 21–2
'MeToo' movement 31
ministers 2, 4
Ministry of Defence 2
monarchy
    governments 1
    role of 38–9
    Royal Assent 6
    royal prerogative 4
Money Bills 8
motions 41
MPs (Members of Parliament) 4, 41
    debating 10
    see also elections

N
National Assembly for Wales 25
New Zealand 39
Nicaragua 33
non-departmental public bodies
    (NDPBs) 2
non-ministerial departments 2
Nordic countries, women's political
    representation 35
Northern Ireland, devolved government
    2, 3, 9
Northern Ireland Act 1998 9
Northern Ireland Assembly 25
Northern Ireland Executive 9

O
Obama, Barack 17
Opposition, the 41

P
Pakistan 36
Parliament 2, 3, 41
    Acts of 3, 6–8, 41
    Bills 6–8, 41
    ceremonial mace 12–13
    composition of 4
    and constitutional law 4
    debating 10
    Draft Bills 3, 6
    functions of 4
    House of Commons 2, 4–7, 10,
        12–14
    House of Lords 2, 4–7, 11

motions 41
MPs (Members of Parliament) 4
sovereignty 4, 38–9
two-House system 5
women in 34–5
Parliament Act 1911 8
Parliament Act 1949 8
pressure groups 4, 6
Prime Minister 2
proportional representation 41
Public Accounts Committee 4
public bodies 2

Q
Queen, role of 38–9
Queen's Speech 6

R
Reform Act 1832 14–15
Representation of the People Act 1918 15
republic governments 1
right to vote 20
Royal Assent 6, 41
royal prerogative 4
Rwanda 34

S
Saudi Arabia 36
Scotland, devolved government 2, 3, 9
Scotland Act 1998 9
Scottish National Party 9
Scottish Parliament 25
secondary legislation 8
Secretaries of State 2
Serbia 33
Sergeant at Arms 12
Single Transferable Vote (STV) 25
Speaker, of the Commons 10, 12–14
Statutory Instruments (SIs) 8
suffrage 15, 30, 36
Supplementary Vote (SV) 25

T
transgender, voting 36
two-House system 5

U
Uganda 33
uncodified constitution 4
United States of America
    and democracy 33
    government 37–9

V
Vatican City 36
voting
    abstaining 19
    age 21–3
    compulsory 16–17
    gender imbalance in 36
    history of 14–15
    mandatory voter identification 18
    manipulation of 29
    right to vote 20
    systems 24–5
    and women 15, 30, 36

W
Wales, devolved government 2, 3, 9
White Papers 6
William of Orange 14
women
    in Parliament 34–5
    suffrage 15, 30, 36
Women's Equality Party 31
World War I 15

Z
Zimbabwe 33

Acknowledgements

The publisher is grateful for permission to reproduce the material in this book. While every care has been taken to trace and acknowledge copyright, the publisher tenders its apology for any accidental infringement or where copyright has proved untraceable. The publisher would be pleased to come to a suitable arrangement in any such case with the rightful owner.

Images

Cover image courtesy of iStock. All other images courtesy of Unsplash and Pixabay.

Illustrations

Don Hatcher: pages 3 & 18. Simon Kneebone: pages 5 & 26. Angelo Madrid: pages 24 & 38.

Additional acknowledgements

With thanks to the Independence team: Shelley Baldry, Danielle Lobban, and Jan Sunderland.

Tracy Biram

Cambridge, September 2019